Heart-warming tales of canine companionship from celebrities and other extraordinary people

My Dog, my Friend

Hubble & Hattie

All author royalties donated to SAMARITANS

A registered charity 219432

Compiled by **Jacki Gordon**

The Hubble & Hattie imprint was launched in 2009 and is named in memory of two very special Westie sisters owned by Veloce's proprietors.
Since the first book, many more have been added to the list, all with the same underlying objective: to be of real benefit to the species they cover, at the same time promoting compassion, understanding and co-operation between all animals (including human ones!)
Hubble & Hattie is the home of a range of books that cover all-things animal, produced to the same high quality of content and presentation as our motoring books, and offering the same great value for money.

More titles from Hubble and Hattie

© Pets as Therapy, Paws for Progress, Portador, Ted Baker PLC, Jackie Kay, Jacki Gordon, Alan Titchmarsh, Antony Worrall Thompson, Ben Rimalower, Bob Alper, Robert Vetere, Brix Smith-Start, Marion Janner, Clare Allan, David Belcher, David Shrigley, Charlie Dimmock, David Blunkett, William McIlvanney, Edward Stourton, Esther Rantzen, Fidelma Cook, Fred MacAulay, Glyn Jones, Helen FitzGerald, Ian Hamilton, Jenni Murray, John Hegley, Jon Landau, Julie Myerson, Lynne Truss, Emma Chichester Clark, Tony Roper, Rankin, Stephen Platt, Marty Becker, Matthew Offord, Melanie Reid, Mohamed Al Fayed, Nanette Mutrie, Richard Holloway, Sally Beamish, Simon Callow, Stanley Coren, Steve Trigg, Tim Dowling, Jude Brooks & Veloce Publishing Ltd 2014.

Saturday 30 May 2009 from Diary of a Dog-Walker: Time Spent Following a Lead by Edward Stourton, published by Doubleday. Reprinted by permission of The Random House Group Limited.

Front cover image of Lynne Truss and Hoagy courtesy Vybarr Cregan-Reid. Back cover images courtesy (top row; l-r): Paul Scala, Pete Bartlett, Rankin, Amy Clarke; (bottom row; l-r): uncredited, Lionel Trudel, Tom Kidd, uncredited. Cutout image courtesy Andrew Tannahill.

For post publication news, updates and amendments relating to this book please visit www.hubbleandhattie.com/extras/HH4610

www.hubbleandhattie.com

First published in September 2014 by Veloce Publishing Limited, Veloce House, Parkway Farm Business Park, Middle Farm Way, Poundbury, Dorchester, Dorset, DT1 3AR, England. Fax 01305 250479/e-mail info@hubbleandhattie.com/web www.hubbleandhattie.com.
ISBN: 978-1-845846-10-7UPC: 6-36847-04610-1.

Contents

Dedications and acknowledgements

Dedication
To Looka, who introduces joy to every day

Looka's dedication
To Kirsty – my cup runneth over every Friday

Acknowledgements
This book could never have come about without the support of many, many people. First of all, I would like to thank all the wonderful contributors. They have bounded on board and buoyed me with their support. I want to acknowledge their fabulously helpful agents and managers, too – vital links in the chain. I have also had outstanding support from people working for, or with, third sector organisations in obtaining accounts from individuals whom their charities support: Rebecca Leonardi (Paws for Progress); Holly Yuille and Liz Edwards (The Big Issue Foundation); Myrid Ramsay (Canine Partners), and Dinah Baynton-Dibley and Andrea Whitwham (both Pets as Therapy).

Steve Platt, in his roles as Samaritans trustee, valued colleague and fun friend, has provided instrumental and jovial support throughout this project.

Appreciative thanks go to Jude Brooks, the publisher – like me, a strong woman. I think we made a good team.

Family, friends and fellow dog owners in the park have not only put up with my obsession with this project for a very long time, they have offered me suggestions for contributors. All of you will be invited to my book launch party so that I can hug you in person, and we can

My Dog, my Friend

crack open the bubbly stuff. Norma and Kenny Morrison, Avril Blamey and Lisa Cohen – I know that you'll be first over the threshold!

There are some, however, who deserve special mention here, and chief among these are: Dawn Griesbach, work associate and now a fellow dog-owning consultant and friend, whose great ideas just kept coming and coming; my longstanding and dear friend Jan Cassidy, who totally 'got' my idea from the start and has provided enthusiastic encouragement throughout – when walking her big, black, doleful-eyed Labradoodle, Paddy; during our long chats at the corner of our streets, and over our far-too-infrequent glasses of wine, dinners, or trips to the cinema; Cathi Rimalower, who lives too far away, yet has been hugely interested and supportive, wherever in the world we have had a chance to meet up, and who gave me a tremendous lead; Katherine O'Donnell (the world is a better place for having women like her in it), and Sergio Casci (talented, good-looking,

and oh-so-modest with it!) for their introductions to great people in their respective little black books. And Andrew Tannahill for taking photos of Looka (a challenging feat as she's a constantly moving target) and me (a reluctant model), and not only capturing Looka's beauty but, amazingly, managing to make me look better than I do in real life.

My immediate family has been brilliant, as always – embracing my dogginess and dogged determination to compile *My Dog, my Friend* – my son, Tim Gordon; my mum, Joan Rodney, and Philip and Cherie Rodney, Marie Sluglett, and Lisa Barnett.

And then there's Paul (Van Dryver), my partner, who I love dearly (despite his annoying ways). He makes me laugh (even first thing in the morning); supports me in everything I do (apart from my forays into violin 'playing' and tap dancing – inadvisable as these may have been), and, best of all, has learned to share his toys with our lovely Looka.

Jacki Gordon, Glasgow

5

© Jacki Gordon

Foreword

Stephen Platt

I am delighted to have been asked to write a foreword to this collection of entertaining, moving and enlightening accounts of the joys and challenges of being a dog owner. The contributions illustrate in many, varied ways the key role played by dogs in enhancing our emotional wellbeing. As a trustee of Samaritans and long-time researcher with a keen interest in understanding the factors that promote and endanger mental health and ill-health, I value very greatly the learning and comfort that this collection offers, not just to those who are dog lovers or owners, but also to those who may be sceptical about the benefits of dog ownership.

According to conventional wisdom, owning a pet – and especially a dog – is beneficial to human health and wellbeing. The reader may be surprised to learn that there is also copious supporting evidence from a considerable body of scientific research which reaches the same conclusion.

The inclusion of animals in therapeutic activities, known as animal-assisted intervention (AAI), has been suggested as a treatment for emotionally-impaired children, such as those affected by autism spectrum disorder (ASD). Improvements have been reported for many areas of functioning known to be impaired in ASD, including social interaction, communication, problem behaviours, autistic severity, and stress. Horses are often used to improve muscle tone and motor skills in children with cerebral palsy, and in persons who suffer from painful spasms in their lower limbs. Dogs have been shown to be able to assist people with various disabilities in performing everyday activities, thus reducing their dependence on others.

There is evidence that dog therapy benefits older people with dementia living in residential aged care facilities. During dog contact, social behaviour improves, while agitated and aggressive behaviour decreases, and overall functioning is enhanced. As an additional treatment approach in psychiatric settings, AAI has been thoroughly explored and shown to improve the socialisation of psychiatric patients, help to restore and maintain their independence, and provide a wide range of psychological benefits. More general therapeutic outcomes associated with AAI are: enhanced socialisation, reduction of stress, anxiety and loneliness, improvement in mood and general wellbeing, and development of leisure and recreation skills.

There is some research support for dogs' ability to detect ill-health in humans, specifically cancer, epileptic seizures, and hypoglycaemia. The presence of a pet at home may help to develop children's social skills. Dog owners are more physically active and have lower blood pressure and plasma cholesterol, as well as lower susceptibility to mental stress.

Studies have shown a positive relationship between pet ownership and health (including mental health) for populations facing considerable challenges. For example, pet ownership has been associated with: higher survival rates following a heart attack, lower rates of depression among HIV+ men, and reduced doctors' visits among the elderly.

A recent article examining the consequences of pet ownership among a community sample concluded that dogs and other pets can serve as important sources of social support, and provide many positive and physical benefits for their owners: when compared to non-owners, pet owners had higher self-esteem, greater levels of exercise and physical fitness, tended to be less lonely and less fearful, and were more extrovert and less preoccupied. Importantly, too, the authors concluded that pet owners were "just as close" to key people in their lives as were non-owners. Thus, there was no evidence that owners' relationships with their pets "came at the expense" of human relationships. In fact, having a pet was found to complement human sources of social support.

Why might people benefit from pet ownership? One possibility is that pets constitute an important source of social support. There is ample research

© Claudia Martin

Stephen with his 'nephew,' Buster

evidence that both psychological and physical health are affected by the quantity and quality of social support: 'better' social support leads to 'better' health.

Readers of this collection may not be aware that all royalties are being donated to Samaritans. Jacki Gordon, the compiler, and all contributors have given their services for free – Samaritans tend to evoke this kind of generous response – and maybe it would be helpful to provide some information about this exceptional organisation.

Since 1953, Samaritans has provided a confidential emotional support service for people in the UK and

My Dog, my Friend

Ireland who are experiencing distress or having suicidal thoughts and feelings. Its mission is to reduce the incidence of suicidal feelings and behaviour, leading to fewer deaths by suicide. Apart from being available 24/7 by phone, email, letter, SMS and face-to-face, Samaritans also work in the local community, visiting schools, prisons and workplaces, often in partnership with other organisations, agencies and experts, and seeks to influence public policy on suicide prevention. Samaritans' services are delivered by more than 20,000 highly trained and committed volunteers, organised in 201 local branches, who are contacted in excess of five million times each year.

Samaritans' service is built upon several important values that are central to how support is delivered: listening, because exploring feelings alleviates distress and helps people to reach a better understanding of their situation and the options open to them; confidentiality, because if people feel safe they are more likely to be open about their feelings; people making their own decisions, because people have the right to find their own solution, and telling people what to do takes responsibility away from them; being non-judgemental, because people should be able to talk to us without fear of prejudice or rejection, and human contact, because giving people time, undivided attention and empathy meets a fundamental emotional need and reduces distress and despair.

What is striking from the contributions in this book is the myriad ways that dogs support us, although not by offering a telephone helpline service …

For more information, you can visit http://www.samaritans.org/

Stephen Platt recently retired as Professor of Health Policy Research at the University of Edinburgh. He has published extensively on suicidal behaviour, and was co-editor, with Jacki Gordon, of the International Handbook of Suicide Prevention. *His childhood was enlivened by the psychopathic behaviour of the family's pet Corgi (named Bimbo)!*

On the origins of the pieces

Jacki Gordon

My story about this book has a number of origins. The first of these was a newspaper column by journalist Melanie Reid that I read many years ago. Now, I would say Melanie Reid, *the* journalist – but more about that in a minute.

The article in question was just 150 or so words and, torn out of the *Glasgow Herald*, remained pinned to my fridge for a long time. It survived a house move and was transferred to its new fridge door for several more years, where it became horribly dog-eared (no pun intended). I then copied it out for posterity. The writing was a stunning evocation of horses: their magnificence and their smell, powerfully rekindling and flooding me with memories of my happy teens spent at the nearby stables.

Fast forward a few years to when my partner, Paul, and I went to the Isle of Mull for my 50th birthday. Paul is very good at surprises – good surprises, that is – and, after booking into the hotel and depositing our bags in our room, he began to bustle me out the door. He seemed to be doing so for a reason, and there, sitting right outside the bedroom, was a broken-coated Lurcher. My dream dog! This truly was the best of surprises.

I turned to Paul, and, in that moment, I could see his brain working –

click, click, click – and he started to shake his head. "He's not yours," he said.

Hughie the Lurcher belonged to Julia and Matthew Reade, owners of Calgary Farmhouse, just a short walk from the idyllic white sandy beach to which Paul had been trying to hurry me. Over the course of those few days in Mull, I was consumed with thoughts of getting my very own Hughie, and talked to Julia and Matthew – too much, I suspect – about this. There was one problem. I was out all day, Monday to Friday, at work, and could not provide a good home for a dog.

My work at the time was in the Scottish Government, where I was responsible for improving evidence on suicide prevention, and then helping policy planners and practitioners understand the implications of that evidence. Without a doubt, it was an important area of work. I would get up at 6.15, go to the gym, spend a long day at work, and return home 12 hours later, exhausted.

I had always expected to be living my life differently at 50. And I *wanted* to be living my life differently.

I resigned from my job to go freelance and work from home. Sorry, I resigned from my job to go freelance *in order that* I could work from home.

9

My Dog, my Friend

Convincing Paul that having a dog was the only sure-fire way to ensure I would take breaks from sitting in front of my computer, I reserved a puppy for bringing home a week later …

Enter Looka (short for "Look Ah've got a Lurcher at last"). She is my dearest friend – who else would lie on their back, paws in the air, and keep me company as I am bent over my computer, and then, when it is time, jolt me out of my work and take me out for long walks, gifting precious time for me to lope along and reconnect with life beyond work.

My lovely Looka cheers me when I need cheering, and even when I don't. Her wide-mouthed smile enchants, and her good humour is a constant – a rare quality in any human (and I most certainly include myself in that). She is my number one fan and I am hers.

It shames me but, pre-Looka, I knew only the neighbours on each side of the house where we live, whereas now, thanks to our three-times-a-day walks, I feel that I'm part of the local community. And that community is not just people with dogs, as having Looka at my side leads to conversations with people, young and old, every day. We talk about dogs. We talk about anything and everything.

My mum is a very spritely woman who we call on to dog-sit from time to time. When out walking Looka, the invisibility that she suffers as an older person is replaced by friendly chats with people who know Looka, and with people who don't. For Mum, these dog-walking fringe benefits more than compensate for the early morning wake-up licks and her bag-and-scooper responsibilities.

• Fact – dogs can enhance our lives. And they can do so significantly.
• Fact – dogs can make us feel better in and about ourselves; they can be good for our health, including our mental wellbeing.

The idea kept nagging away at me – wouldn't it be great to compile a collection of accounts about the positive impact that dogs have on our lives, including our mental health, and raise money for charity at the same time? Having worked in the mental health field for a long time – and being well aware of the good work that the charity does – the Samaritans was an obvious choice. But what would prompt people buy a book such as this? If the accounts were well-written, maybe …? Just like, for example, the horsey piece that Melanie Reid had penned, and which I still had.

I sounded out some close friends, and was buoyed by their positive response to the idea of an anthology of how dogs enrich our lives. An early supporter was Professor Stephen Platt – colleague, friend, fellow co-editor on a previous book, and a Samaritans trustee – who enthusiastically agreed to help. I knew it would be important for prospective contributors to understand that 100% of the royalties for this book had been signed over to Samaritans, and Steve was the linchpin in liaising with Samaritans and obtaining endorsement of the whole project from its Chief Executive, Catherine Johnstone

Getting a book published – in particular a collection like this – I found to be a chicken-and-egg affair, and many

My Dog, my Friend

would-be contributors wanted to know details about the book before agreeing to write a piece; yet I needed contributor names to convince a prospective publisher that my idea had wings and would fly …

And so I began firing off emails to people who are known to write well, requesting support in principle for my book proposal if I should find a publisher for it. Fidelma Cook was my first 'yes,' and her warm response gave me a glimmer of hope. After hers, slowly but surely, the 'yeses' started to trickle in, and I began to believe that the book would actually happen.

With great trepidation, I wrote to Melanie Reid. Besides being an award-winning journalist, she was part of the story behind this book, and so I really wanted her on board. However, I knew that, daily, she battles to get her own writing done, following a fall from her horse in 2010, when she broke her neck and back. The obstacles she faces in her daily life are huge, and although her tenacity is inspirational, her recovery is achingly slow. I was overjoyed when her "How could I say no?" appeared in my inbox.

Once I had about twenty people agreeing in principle to contribute to the book, I looked for a publisher who I hoped would have an affinity with what I was trying to do. I came across Hubble and Hattie, with its commitment to foster animal understanding and compassion, and my speculative email met with an immediate reply. As a former Samaritan and besotted dog owner, Hubble and Hattie's proprietor, Jude Brooks, totally understood what I was trying to achieve. A contract followed just a few days later.

I got back in touch with the wonderful people who had agreed to support the book at the earliest stages, and wrote to others requesting a contribution. My dog-owning friends and work associates fed me lots of suggestions about who I might approach, and even my non-dog-minded friends 'nominated' potential contributors.

Each and every 'yes' elicited an ecstatic response from me – air-punching, a jig danced in front of my PC – and always an excited text to Paul, to my wonderful son, Tim, and to whoever had suggested the contributor in the first place.

Then and now, I am extremely grateful for every piece that has been donated to this book in order to celebrate dogs and what they do for us, and to raise funds for Samaritans.

As for the book title, at one point, inspired by contributor Lynne Truss' book about punctuation, *Eats Shoots and Leaves*, I wanted to call this collection *Eats, Pants and Poos*. But dogs do so very much more for us than that, which includes preventing us from sitting at our computers for too long.

Now, where is that lead …?

Jacki would like to spend all her time enjoying Looka. Unfortunately, pesky work gets in the way – providing planning and evaluation consultancy support to services and projects that are seeking to improve the health and wellbeing of the two-legged population. Jacki is co-editor of two previous publications: How We Feel: an insight into the emotional world of teenagers, *and* The International Handbook of Suicide Prevention: research, policy and practice.

Helping us with life: Plum has the solution

Truly amazing creatures
Rankin

Throughout my life, I have always owned dogs. At the moment I have three: Tombi, Pickle and Beans.

At 13 years old, Tombi the Jack Russell is the leader of the pack and a bit of a grump. My wife, Tuuli, has owned her since she was 18. Pickle is a four-year-old Lurcher who we rescued from the RSPCA. He's called that because he wasn't in the best of conditions when they found him. And then there's Beans. At just over a year old she's an incredibly gentle Whippet and a natural born model! She's the baby of our pack. We rescued her from a charity called the Greyhound Gap and she was so small that they used a can of beans to show her size in a photograph … hence the name.

With both my studio and house in the same building in North London, I am constantly at work. I lead a really busy life and am always travelling for shoots. Having the dogs to come home to is a great stress reliever; they're always pleased to see you. They're a great distraction from even the most hectic days, and I can't imagine my home without them.

The dogs also inject a bit of fun into proceedings. They are all regulars in the studio – especially Beans. I've included her in various shoots with Tuuli, and she even starred in a new campaign for Jigsaw. Not only is my Instagram feed littered with images of them (watch out for the one of Beans dressed up as Dobby The House Elf), but I actually photograph the whole pack each year for our dog calendar. It's something that's really close to my family's hearts. So far we've done a horoscope-themed calendar, Dogue (doggy *Vogue*), and last year's was films – for example *The Grrrraduate*.

Whenever I can I try to help raise awareness about the benefits of owning dogs. I recently did a shoot for Dogs Trust to highlight the number of animals who are abandoned each year. We took photos of rescued dogs and their owners, and it was so clear to me how much these once discarded dogs had changed the lives of their new families. It's amazing how much love a dog has to give, even if they have had a hard start in life.

They are truly amazing creatures and we could all learn a thing or two from them.

Rankin with Beans, Tombi and Pickle

Possibly best known as the photographer of very, very famous people, such as Madonna, David Bowie, the Rolling Stones, and Peter Capaldi, amongst others, Rankin cannot be pigeonholed quite so easily. When he was interviewed on BBC Radio 4's Desert Island Discs, Kirsty Young introduced him thus:

"He started out doing fashion shoots, and is very good at making pretty young things look even prettier. But his work and influence have spread well beyond the glossy pages of style bibles. Rankin went to college to study accountancy – but his head was turned in his halls of residence where the art students seemed to be having all the fun. Within a few years Kate Moss was posing for him in nothing but a fedora and leather boots. However, his reputation for raunch was placed firmly on the back burner the day he photographed Her Majesty The Queen: his picture of a serene and smiling monarch now hangs in The National Portrait Gallery."

My dogs, my pressure valves

Antony Worrall Thompson

It is well documented that, in 2012, I had what can only be described as a mental breakdown. I wasn't in a very good place early that year, and during that time was grateful for the support of my friends and family. And classed as family were – and still are – my two faithful dogs, Flossie, a Black Russian Terrier, and Rodney, a Golden Retriever. We've had them since they were puppies.

During the time I was seeking professional treatment, I found strength and solace walking both of them by our local lake in Oxfordshire, and for them being a constant in what was a pretty turbulent time.

Both of them have wonderful temperaments. Rodney is gentle – indeed, a gentleman of the dog world; Flossie is a little more exuberant and a perfect foil for Rodney.

It's said that walking is good for the soul and, indeed, for your health, so I consider my walks with the dogs a real benefit to my wellbeing. As a chef and restaurateur, I live a high-pressured life, and these dogs are my pressure valve: my release. When my wife, Jay, and I walk the dogs along the Thames riverbanks or local lakes, it is one of my pleasures (and indeed, theirs!).

Our children adore them – they've always grown up with dogs around them.

We encourage dogs and well-behaved children at The Greyhound, the pub and restaurant Jay and I run, near Henley-on-Thames. It's delightful to see the bond that dogs have with their owners – all shapes and sizes from the bouncy terrier to the stately Old English.

Every loving home needs a dog – and every dog needs a loving home …

Antony and Jay with Rodney

Embarking on his career, Antony Worrall Thompson's final report from his hotel management degree, forty years ago, read: "On no account should this boy be let loose near a kitchen." From these inauspicious beginnings, Antony went on to become an award-winning restaurateur, a long-standing and much-loved regular television presenter, newspaper columnist, and prolific cookbook writer! Awtrestaurants.com/Awtonline.co.uk

Lulu

Alan Titchmarsh

Her name was Lulu. Not my choice: I'd have preferred something manly like 'Jess.' I decided we'd change her name after we'd adopted her at the age of two, from someone who was attached to the foreign office and leaving the country. But her behaviour (in our tiny three-up, three-down terrace house) was such in the first few weeks that a change of name seemed like just another obstacle.

The house was very small, and she was a yellow Labrador. She wasn't particularly *bad*, as such, just full of beans, boisterous – and the only thing she had been taught to do properly was chase cats. We already had a cat. It was not an easy transition for her (or the cat), and after six weeks we went round to the friends of the folk who had moved, courtesy of the foreign office, and confessed that we had bitten off more than we could chew (not a problem that Lulu ever experienced).

They poured us a glass of wine and listened patiently to our tale of woe. "Give her another week" they said.

We went home despondent. The following morning Lulu was a changed dog. Imagination? Well, you could say that, but we reckon she simply detected something in the air and decided that she'd better fit in. Not that she lost her spirit – far from it – but she certainly became more accommodating; even of the cat, Chloe.

I walked her, trained her rather more, and took her on adventures. We climbed Great Gable together, though I did have to carry her up the last fifty yards since her claws would give her no purchase on the rocky crag. Once there she proceeded to demolish the picnics of other climbers – to their amusement and my embarrassment. On the way down, her appetite unsated, she would devour ... well, anything she considered edible, really, but I won't go into that: it's a classic Labrador trait ...

On visits to Yorkshire to see my parents, she would swim out into the centre of the River Wharfe, face upstream, and tread water for half an hour while onlookers on the bank would exhort us to rescue her. It wasn't necessary: she came back when she was ready.

When the children came along she was the perfect household pet; they learned to walk, holding on to her back. As she grew older we dreaded the day when we would be without her, and so we decided to have an overlap.

We acquired two eight-week-old yellow Labs – sisters. Their grandfather had been bred at Sandringham, and so we called them Grace and Favour. Lulu took one look at them and thought "If you think I'm going to die you've got another think coming." She lived on for another five years. I would roll on the floor with her in mock fights and she would growl playfully like a lion, with the softest of mouths. We would lie together on the grass in the garden – my head resting on her ribcage. She liked that.

All three dogs are no longer with us and our aged second cat – Spud, a black-and-white Postman-Pat cat – would not take kindly to another dog. But when Spud is no longer with us (another thought I can't bear), I'd like to think that we might ... well, I know I'll never find another Lulu.

We never did get round to calling her Jess, but then neither did we call her Lulu: she was always, quite simply, Loo. I gaze fondly at her photograph every morning when I get dressed. She was, without doubt, the dog of my life.

Alan Titchmarsh is a well-known face and voice on television and radio as a gardening expert, interviewer and presenter. Notable highlights in his career include writing the fastest-selling gardening book of all time; designing a garden for Nelson Mandela, and being immortalised as a wax statue in Madame Tussaud's! In the 2000 New Year Honours List, Alan was appointed MBE for services to horticulture and broadcasting. He lives in Hampshire (and the Isle of Wight) with his wife and assorted livestock.

Ten out of Ten

Lynne Truss

There is a 'blind date' feature in *The Guardian* magazine every Saturday, which I read with grim fascination, partly because the outcome is nearly always the same. The people meet, and afterwards they answer questions. In the replies, the boy invariably says that the girl was great, and that her table manners were impeccable. He gives her 7 out of ten, and says he'd like to meet her again, "but only as friends." The girl generally comes across as insufferably self-confident, and is a bit rude about the boy, but will likewise approve his table manners (I don't know why they keep asking the question, actually), and say he'd be nice to have for a friend.

Every week, I ask myself, "Why do I read this thing?" And then I realise it's because I understand the inherent problem. These people are all looking for the wrong things in a partner. If compatibility is such a paramount issue, why don't they all get a dog?

Perhaps it's just that the two things coincided for me so neatly. For twenty years (aged 31 to 51) I had cats, and coincidentally throughout those decades I held out hope of meeting the perfect man. Then I switched to having Hoagy the Norfolk Terrier, and instantly found absolute peace and happiness. *Would*

I introduce Hoagy to my friends? What, are you kidding? My friends all adore Hoagy, and I suspect many of them now come mainly to see him rather than me. *Would I introduce Hoagy to my parents?* Of course. My mum adores him. *What do you and Hoagy talk about?* Anything and everything. He is incredibly sympathetic and supportive to my views on all matters. *Table manners OK?* Sadly, his eating happens much too quickly for me to judge, but I'll say they're great anyway. *Will I see him again?* I already see him all day, every day! *Marks out of ten?* 10!

It's the first question in the questionnaire that's the most interesting to me now. They always ask the participants, "What did you expect?" But it's hard to think back. I keep trying to remember what it was like when I first met Hoagy (or Hovis, as he was named by the breeder). At the time, he was 14 months old, and we met in the kitchen of the breeder's house. He stood on his back legs a lot and made frantic importuning movements that broke my heart. I picked him up and he licked my face.

Three weeks later, I went back with a friend and collected him – but it was a huge step to take. I didn't know him at all. In advance of getting him, I bought lots of standard doggy things that proved

Lynne and Hoagy

completely superfluous to requirements – tennis balls, squeaky toys, big wire cage, and so on. It turned out that Hoagy's sole interests in life are sniffing, weeing, eating, being patted by strangers, and sniffing and weeing a bit more. When I did misguidedly place him in the cage, on his very first bedtime, it made him howl so desperately that I never put him in it again.

"First impressions?" That's the other question in *The Guardian*, and this one's very easy because Hoagy makes an incredibly good first impression on everyone. As we walk along – me, this lumbering, middle-aged woman in bad

My Dog, my Friend

clothes; he, this tiny cheerful animal trotting at my side with his tail wagging – all I see is people breaking into smiles. He is simply an adorable dog, and he makes the world a nicer place. He loves to say hello. True, he loses interest in people quite quickly, but – well, it's like the bit in *The Talented Mr Ripley* about the fickleness of Dickie Greenleaf (Jude Law): "When he's paying attention to you, it's like the sun shines on you, and it's glorious," says Dickie's love-crazy girlfriend (Gwyneth Paltrow). "And then he forgets you and it's very, very cold."

God knows, of course, what Hoagy would say about me. Marks out of ten? About six, I expect. I never met his friends or his parents; as for conversation, he doesn't really care what we talk about as long as it has the words "treat" and "breakfast" in it somewhere. No, I admit it's all a bit one-way if you take the 'blind date' model for the relationship. But I still think ours is more satisfactory than the ones between youthful (but sassy) systems analysts and events co-ordinators, whose main problem (in my opinion) is that they've met far too many people in their lives already.

By the way, I think I can guess what Hoagy would reply to the question about table manners. He wouldn't waste time with all that 'impeccable' nonsense. "Table manners? What are you talking about? I just want her to put the damned plate down so I can lick it clean!"

Lynne Truss is best known for her bestselling book on punctuation, Eats, Shoots & Leaves. *She has written novels, short stories and plays. Her latest book, published in 2014, is a comic-horror novella entited* Cat Out of Hell.

© Vybarr Cregan-Reid

Gladys and Pixie

An interview with Brix Smith-Start

Jacki
Brix, have you always been a dog person?

Brix
I've always been an animal person. Animals have always been my closest friends and companions since as long as I can remember, and, yeah, I've been particularly close to dogs.

Jacki
And why did you decide to get your Pugs, Gladys and Pixie?

Brix
Well, I've had many dogs throughout my life and I remember once, when – I think it was in 1981 – my parents took me and my sisters on a trip to Europe, and we came to London … they took us to London, Paris and Venice, and we'd never been away from America, and I loved London; straight away I knew, I had this feeling when we were there, and I remember seeing this elderly gentleman walking down the street on a hot summer's day with two Pugs, and I'd never seen a Pug in my life. I didn't know what they were, and I saw these two Pugs panting and straining at the lead with curling tongues and bulging eyes, and they were so cute that I remember falling to my knees in

front of the man and his dogs and going "Oh my god, they are the cutest thing I've ever seen!" And the man was quite dismissive – he was really posh, you know, it was somewhere in Chelsea I think it was – and he was like "Oh my god, this crazy American child!" But years later when I was with Nigel Kennedy, we were looking through *Vogue* magazine and there was this article on Valentino the designer and all his Pugs, and I started freaking out and I said "Oh my god, Nigel, those were the dogs I saw! Those were the dogs! What are they?" and he said "Oh they're Pugs," and he bought me my first Pug. And I've had Pugs now for 25 years.

Jacki
What difference have Gladys and Pixie made to your life?

Brix
I don't even know how to quantify a response to that kind of a question because they simply just bring me so much joy, it's, like, incalculable. I don't even know the word to even say how much it is! Basically, dogs do so much for you. I mean I don't even know where to start. The first thing is, they show us how to be better people by showing us unconditional love, which

My Dog, my Friend

is something that humans don't do naturally, unfortunately: dogs do. Dogs never hold a grudge – they're always happy to see you whether you're five minutes out of the house or two hours; they're grateful, eternally grateful for food, for love, you know. They're just really incredible creatures. The other thing is, people don't realise that dogs are intelligent on a level that I believe is more intelligent than humans, because I believe that they actually function on many different levels. They see things that we don't see; they sense things; they hear things more clearly; they smell to a degree that we have no conception of. They can smell if somebody's ill. They can understand depression without speaking. They can read human behaviour. I mean, people say "I wish my dog could speak," well, to me the dogs can speak, because they can read everything and respond to everything that you're doing on so many levels, on levels that we possibly never could, and I think they're so underestimated, their intelligence, you know, I think scientists are only now really finding out the depth of, like, the intelligence of these animals.

Jacki
Tell me about Gladys and Pixie.

Brix
I've got Gladys right next to me. Yeah. I mean Gladys … is an incredible creature. She … I mean they're both incredible, and they're both completely different in personality, you know, as different as you and I, but Gladys has this seriously developed sixth sense about people and their energy, so … this dog is, like, docile, if you've ever seen her she's like butter, you know, I would take her on

TV and we'd do an episode of *Gok's Fashion Fix* and she would be in front of three thousand screaming people in a shopping mall on-stage, and she would be asleep in my arms, she's just so relaxed. But if we're in the street and somebody comes near me and something's wrong with that person in terms of 1) their energy is wrong, 2) they might be on drugs, 3) they're angry: whatever it is, the dog will let me know. It's really interesting. So Gladys literally looks after me physically, and Pixie looks after me mentally. They have two jobs!

Jacki
Can you say a little bit about how Pixie looks after you mentally?

Brix
Yeah. Pixie's the most sweetest, happiest, loveliest girl, and if you've had a hard day; you're a bit low, she'll just run to you with a present in her mouth, anything, like loads of different toys and things, she'll grab something, even if it's a pen, a postage stamp, a piece of cardboard, and she'll run around and circle you with such joy, that for that minute you've forgotten about what's happened and you're just so happy. She just lifts your spirit and brings you literally into the now, and when you're in the now you're not worrying about the past or the future. She's amazing.

    I want to tell you, every night, my husband and I and Gladys and Pixie all go to sleep in the same bed, and my husband goes to sleep with his arms around Gladys, and Pixie goes to sleep against my side, and that is it. I love that because it's so comforting and I feel safe and I know that if there's a noise outside, or anybody anywhere, we're just safe, they'll let us know.

© Paul Scala

Brix with Gladys and Pixie

US-born Brix Smith-Start is one of the most recognized faces in fashion. Brix lives in London with her husband – fashion mogul Philip Start – and her two pugs, Gladys and Pixie.

25

Buddy

Marion Janner

Let's start with introductions, albeit rather unidirectional.

Hello. I'm Buddy, a youthful, laidback, somewhat daft Tibetan Terrier. I was rescued at six months from a breeder, and the risk of a lifetime of being primped and preened for dog shows. Instead, I've become a UK pioneer as a mental health support dog. Not the first and, though I say so myself, not the smartest (in any sense), but a devoted and docile companion.

And now let me introduce my human, Marion, a 54-year-old north Londoner. She's very short. Really very short indeed. Yup, that's pretty much it. Oh right. She also dabbles in stand-up comedy, gardening, and parenting, and spends absurd amounts of time on her computer doing goodness knows what.

I let her come with me everywhere – it's been Buddy at Butlins, Broadmoor, Brixton Prison, Buckingham Palace, and loads of places which begin with other letters. The best is going on visits to mental health wards. Frankly, I'm a patient magnet, and am usually instantly surrounded by several people with well-honed tummy-rubbing skills. They tell me about their dogs, showing me photos (some are very cool dudes who I'd like to meet and sniff) on their phones or bedroom walls, and say the nicest things about how adorable I am and how much they miss their hairy companions.

Actually, I do tend to attract a lot of attention when we're out and about. Probably my natural charm and effortless good looks, but the neon yellow jacket advertising my support dog role (and therefore Marion's disability) may play a small part. People at bus stops and in shops always ask the same, we think very reasonable, question: "What is a support dog?" Marion replies along the lines of: "I've got a severe mental illness and Buddy is my companion dog, keeping me a bit saner, a bit safer." People often say: "How lovely! Oops! I don't mean being mentally ill is lovely, but, er, it's lovely to have such a great companion." How right they are. They sometimes ask if I'm specially trained and Marion mumbles that I sort of am. Mercifully, I don't need to do anything tricky like fetch her medication, persuade her to pay her bills or the like. It's enough that I'm simply a delight to be with!

Of course, given the whole madness thing, life is pretty difficult for Marion. She has something called Borderline Personality Disorder which, believe me, is anything but borderline! And is a bit rude, really, given that most

My Dog, my Friend

© Christian Sinibaldi

Marion and Buddy

of her personality is neat and friendly! But the BPD does make her very, very sad and despondent, and everyone seems very worried about her safety. Which is where I come in! Marion does have regular meltdowns when we're out and about – but she loves loves loves me and wouldn't put me in any danger. So she somehow manages to stagger on and get me across streets and back home nice and safely. By that time, she's feeling calmer and can ring the Samaritans or one of her therapists.

So that's us! Team Buddy. Keeping Marion going; bringing joy to hundreds of people we meet on mental health wards while maintaining my important role as chief sniffer at our local park.

Marion Janner OBE is mother to a 10-year-old Tibetan Terrier, Buddy. In her spare time between walks, feeds and tummy rubs, she runs Star Wards, which helps mental health wards provide actively therapeutic care for in-patients. The project is based on Marion's deep appreciation of the care she receives at St Ann's Hospital, Tottenham, and possible partly thanks to regular calls with Samaritans.

The dog who could be Graham Norton

Melanie Reid

She came via a re-homing organisation, the Scottish Staffie Rescue. All we knew was that she was timid, 18 months old, brindled black, had already had four different homes, and had been returned to her breeder, who had a premature baby and couldn't keep her. Oh, and that we had to uplift her by the weekend. So we drove four hours and found her, wild as the hills, an unguided missile of muscle, whizzing around the living room of a tiny council house without touching the floor. In the car she was obedient but incredibly vocal, squeaking and squawking and puking – once down the plastic sleeve of the gear lever, but mostly into my lap – all the way home. What else could we call her but Pip Squeal?

It was like the arrival of a damaged foster child: insecure, uncertain, needy, with behaviour patterns that told us she'd had a rotten start. Most of all she needed stability. We were warned she could be pregnant, so she was taken, like a reprobate teenager, for the morning after pill. Then she was spayed. From the start, all Pip was desperate to do was co-operate. With freedom and exercise on the farm, she calmed down (though a serious lesson had to be dealt her after she tried to attack a sheep). She displayed the Staffie's most glorious attributes:

brains; an innate love of people (but not small furry animals; oh no, never), and a magnificent sense of humour. So good-natured is this breed that the Victorians used to call them nanny dogs and leave the children with them. And how traduced their reputation is now by humans.

Ours was a comedian; a maestro; a shameless, guile-filled, lovable, busy-bottomed pocket-rocket. If she was a TV presenter she would be Graham Norton. Just looking at her made us laugh. She never barked or growled; she just released a constant symphony of internal doggy sentiments: yawning, farting, snorting, grunting, yammering, slurping. The belching, though, was the most impressive; when it came to loud, expressive burps, the men of the family respected the fact she made them look amateur. And she talked to us – lip-slapping, plaintive, urgent little sounds, exasperated when we didn't understand. Funniest were her positions: she would pose, simianesque, in her basket, leaning back against the radiator, her front paws reaching up to us for love as we passed, her little pot-belly like a Buddha begging to be stroked. Or she would sit like we'd never seen a dog sit: a winsome tart in a window in the Reeperbahn, slumped back on her tailbone, her legs wide apart

Melanie and Pip

displaying her wares, ears down, eyes sweet and seductive; or she would roll and smile and simultaneously scratch her back and chase her tail, always upside down on the same spot on the living room floor.

And then there was the smile. Oh Lord, this dog had the ugliest, most contorted, submissive, please-love-me smile anyone had ever seen: her upper lip curling up to reveal horrible fangs. She smiled when we returned home; she smiled when we called her; she smiled when she thought we were cross with her. Ours is never a house of conflict; of raised, angry voices, but on the rare occasion someone expressed irritation she would rush, smiling like a dervish, and try and climb into my lap. Someone, earlier in her life, had been verbally violent to her.

Dogs offer deep spiritual comfort, non-judgemental adoration, and a presence that magically lowers human physiological stresses. The inside of their ears smell good, too. And if you need a good, private sob, they keep a secret. All they ask in return is a secure place in the pecking order.

I've spent too much recent time in hospital. Last time I was away, Pip was forlorn, searching the house for me for days. When I did come home, her body language was laugh-out-loud joyous, wriggling around my wheelchair so much she almost turned herself inside out, and smiling so hard I swear her lips met over the top of her muzzle. The most beautiful thing you can ever say to someone is: "You are loved" – but too few people do. Dogs say it to us every day.

Melanie Reid spent most of her life as an award-winning but, happily, rather anonymous journalist with The Times, The Scotsman, The Herald and the Sunday Mail. In 2010 she broke her neck and her back falling off her horse, since when she has written 'Spinal Column' in The Times Saturday magazine, and become famous for being a ridiculously stubborn tetraplegic. In 2011 Melanie won UK Columnist of the Year, which just shows how far you have to go to win one of those things.

She has a husband, a son and a dog, all of them unquantifiably wonderful.

Child substitutes? Of course!

Jenni Murray

I had gone through the worst time of my life by the end of 2006. Both my parents had died, within a few months of each other, ending several years of desperately trying to juggle my responsibilities as a mother, partner, breadwinner and only child. On the day my mother died I was diagnosed with breast cancer, had the necessary surgery, and a long course of debilitating chemotherapy.

And after all this, the house seemed so empty. The children were up and off, and we had no animals apart from an ancient and increasingly stroppy black cat. Our two beloved Miniature Schnauzers, William and Mary, had died a few years earlier from old age. They were both eighteen.

It soon became obvious that what was necessary to cheer things up was a dog, and I found myself scouring the more respectable internet sites that offer puppies for sale.

I was constantly drawn to Chihuahuas, but my older boy, who's a vet, advised against, arguing they tend to be snappy, and citing his profession's dread of any pampered pooch turning up at the surgery in a handbag, and displaying sharp little teeth when approached with a needle.

I ignored him, determined I wanted a dog that would be small enough to transport easily on my weekly commute by train from the Peak District to London and back, and adaptable enough to live a split lifestyle with few opportunities for a long walk.

I found him - my doggy in the window. No more than four weeks old, he was a tiny bundle of adorableness, home bred, with an offer to meet him, his brothers and sisters, and both his parents.

We were drawn to each other immediately: in fact, I would say that, for the first time in my life, I fell in love at first sight. He bounded over to my lap, and was so tiny he happily sat in my hand. My husband, who had not been keen on the tie of a new dog, was charmed from the outset, and joked that he should be named Butch; although he was anything but, the name stuck. I had to wait eight long weeks before I could collect him and bring him home.

Butch changed my life, and is my constant companion. He never complains; never criticises, and is always willing to do whatever I want to do. He mastered the train journey with ease, carefully walking away from the edge of the platform and hopping on and off without fear or complaint. He never travelled in a bag, but on a lead - a proper dog.

My Dog, my Friend

Frida (left) and Butch

We had only one problem. He hated being left alone when I went to work. He cried pitifully: a reminder of the "don't leave me, Mummy" I'd had to steel myself against when the children were small.

I remembered an old vet from way back in my broadcasting career who joined me in local radio for a pet phone-in. He would always advise a second pet – once to cure a masturbating budgie, and then to a clearly house-proud man whose kitten was eating his plants. Six months later this man phoned again to thank James Alcock for his advice, but to let us know he now had two cats eating his plants.

And so came Frida – named for her Mexican predecessor, Frida Kahlo – and as tiny, determined and attention-seeking a creature as you could hope to meet. Butch has the sweetest nature and Frida is unquestionably the boss, but they're affectionate best friends, only falling out over who gets to sit on my lap (both, usually), and who curls up closest in bed. (I know; disgusting, but the best hot water bottles ever.)

I know one shouldn't have a favourite 'child' and I love Frida for her courage, curiosity, independent nature, and ability to become quite demented with excitement. But Butch is steady, protective, supportive, and loves me absolutely unconditionally. He'll always be my Number 1 (sorry, Frida!).

© David Forgham-Bailey

31

Dame Jenni Murray is a big woman, known for her presentation of the BBC Radio programme Woman's Hour, *for hard news and current affairs in television, and articles in a range of newspapers and magazines. But she is soft about her 'babies,' Butch and Frida – Chihuahaus – the smallest, but bravest, of dogs.*

Sometimes, a dog's life turns out to be more interesting than you might think!

David Blunkett

There's an old saying: 'If you want a friend in politics, get a dog.' I have been somewhat luckier than that. Throughout my political life – I've been involved in elected office since 1970 – I've had not only six wonderful dogs, but also more friends than I deserve.

In other words, man's best friends in my case have been both dog and people, but there are some things about a dog that you simply can't fault. They don't argue; they don't make judgements; they may get cheesed off with what you're asking them to do but they don't bear grudges or become spiteful. In other words, they keep their jaws closed, their ears open and, at crucial moments, their tails wagging. (In politics it tends to be the tongue that wags, the jaws that 'jaw' and, as far as the ears are concerned, well!)

My dogs have all been characters. From Ruby, my first and most 'un-guide-dog-like' guide dog, through to my present curly coated Retriever/Labrador cross, Cosby.

Ruby was a pedigree Labrador who, like all Labradors, adored food. But unlike other guide dogs, she appeared to be completely without restraint when it came to not only how *much* she ate but also *what* she ate – with two exceptions. Taking her lead from her master, she turned her nose up at celery! And, it has to be said, with some disgust for a dog in south Yorkshire, eating coal, too.

Otherwise, she would often be found upside down in the dustbin, filled to bursting with rubbish, and extremely smelly for days, happily surviving with goodness knows what inside her!

I knew she was very wily. She could take a trifle off a trolley in the town hall without me noticing, until the crunching sound under the table gave her away (when I was chairing a meeting!). But it was the cries of anguish from small children when we got off a bus, and their ice creams disappeared out of their hands that I remember most. I had to keep a ready supply of coins in my pocket in order to be able to reimburse their parents and smooth over what otherwise would have been an embarrassing incident.

Ruby lived to the ripe old age (for a Labrador) of 16.

After she retired my next dog was Offa, a magnificent German Shepherd/Golden Retriever cross who, sadly, had to retire early because of stomach torsions. Saved by a brilliant vet in Bristol during the course of the 1992 General Election, I don't think it was election campaigning that caused Offa's problems, but rather

My Dog, my Friend

that I'd foolishly let him run about while feeding him when I was on the campaign trail.

Teddy was a magnificent curly coated Retriever/Labrador cross who was very similar to my current dog, and was the first canine to be allowed on the floor of the House of Commons. The 'authorities' asked me whether there was any danger of Teddy causing a disturbance with 'unwarranted noises,' to which I waggishly replied that he could cope with anything in Prime Minister's Questions!

Lucy was a patrician dog: haughty, extremely well behaved, and loved by everybody. She anticipated the 1997 election result back in '94 when, after the European elections – and for reasons entirely beyond me – she decided she'd take me to the Government front bench in the Chamber of the House of Commons, rather than where I was normally seated directly opposite.

My next dog, Sadie (half-sister to Lucy, thanks to the wonders of modern science and artificial insemination), was an excellent guide dog like Lucy, but a little more skittish – her favourite pastime was chasing squirrels. She did, of course, have to take over from Lucy six months into my having become Home Secretary; quite a challenge for a dog: not because of the guiding (as a Cabinet Minister, getting about was not a problem), but because of the stress and strain. But Sadie was popular, and even the staff loved a licked hand and a nose to rub when things were really difficult, and enjoyed the chance of taking her for a walk on what were sometimes 16-hour days; not just for me but some of my private office, too.

And so to Cosby, a massive, 43 kilo,

© Pete Bartlett

David and Cosby

curly coated Retriever/Labrador cross, who is extraordinarily good-natured and wonderful with children, though sharing Ruby's obsession with food slightly. Yes, everything has to be removed from kitchen surfaces and put away, not least because at his height, of course, he can reach just about anything!

Cosby's guiding, his nature, and his general propensity to inspire people to strike up a conversation with me (even if they hate my politics) is both a great advantage and a real icebreaker.

This black curly coated giant of a dog has, like my previous canine partners, his own little quirks in many ways. Not content to simply sleep on one of my

33

My Dog, my Friend

step-daughter's beds, he actually turns down the covers first with his paws. Clever as he is, I've not yet taught him how to read the numbers on the front of buses, or which train platform I need (I do, from time-to-time, get asked this).

Like all dogs, Cosby has to know what's expected of him, and to expect that his owner knows what *he's* doing. Now, there's a thought!

© Hugh Blunkett

David Blunkett is a British Labour politician and a Member of Parliament (MP).

David is blind, and has been from birth, so dogs have been an essential part of his political life, both in terms of 'protecting' him from opponents and winning over the sceptical! There have been times when, as Leader of Sheffield City Council, and later as a Cabinet Minister, David has felt that it was only due to his dog that his sanity was saved!

David's real enjoyment was going into schools with his dogs when he was Education Secretary, and learning about police dogs and what they got up to when he was Home Secretary.

All of the dogs he has had since being elected to Parliament in 1987 have been desperate to get out at the end of the week, which, says David, says more about the Palace of Westminster than it does about the dogs!

Plum
Emma Chichester Clark

I have written and illustrated many children's books over the last twenty-five years, including a series about a Blue Kangaroo, but since the arrival of my dog, Plum, output has begun to dwindle. She took charge of my schedule about four years ago, putting a stop to long hours bent double under the angle-poise, squinting at a shaky line, and dragged me out into the fresh air. Work was no longer seen as a viable excuse to avoid regular exercise or extremes of weather. I wouldn't dream of admitting it to her, but my life and outlook have dramatically improved. And even, perhaps, my sense of humour.

However, as a slave to Plum's ruthless regime, I have also been nagged into spending countless hours illustrating her personal diaries that she has been publishing online in a blog, and there will be a book of her diaries, *PLUMDOG*, published by Jonathan Cape in October 2014.

I've no doubt that I'll be forced to chauffeur her all over the country to promote it, but those of us who have had our day must move over and encourage the young, and I can't help admiring her energy and single-mindedness.

© Rupert Wace

Emma and Plum

Emma has kindly produced the illustration, Helping us with life: Plum has the solution, *which appears on page 13 of this book.*

Hollywood Hounds

Jon Landau

Jon, Julie, Jamie, Jodie … the Landau family. Having recently put to sleep the fifth 'J' of the family – a seven-year-old Leonberger named JJ – something was missing in our home. However, right after JJ lost his battle with cancer, our

Jon and Jango

My Dog, my Friend

thought was that we would not replace him with another dog, but would, instead, take advantage of our new found independence from the responsibilities of being pet owners.

As the days passed I realized more and more the void that had been created. After much discussion between myself and my wife, we decided that with our young adult sons offering to share in the responsibility and commitment that comes with a new dog, we would again bring our family number to five.

We did not want to have a dog from any of the breeds we had had before. We did, however, want another large dog … hopefully, this time one with a longer lifespan than JJ or Jessie, our Bernese Mountain Dog, who we lost to cancer at the age of four. As luck would have it, a litter of Pyrenean Mastiff puppies had recently been birthed at De La Tierra Alta Kennels, just 80 miles

north of our house. We made the drive to learn more about this breed. After an hour-long visit, we were sold. A second trip was required to actually interact with the new litter and pick the puppy we wanted. The vote was unanimous … Male #3.

We waited with great anticipation for the litter to be old enough for us to take home the new addition to our family. As we cradled Male #3 in our arms, he became Jango. The bond was instantaneous; not just with me, but with my wife and sons as well.

Now Jango provides unconditional companionship, whether it be with me when I take him to work; with Jodie when he takes him to class at Cal Arts; with Jamie when he takes him on hikes in the mountains, or with Julie when she takes him to yoga. Jango is the fifth J of our family. (Check him out on his Facebook page: Jango Landau.)

Jon Landau is an Academy Award- and two-time Golden Globe-winning Hollywood film producer. He has produced the world's two highest grossing movies of all time – Avatar and Titanic – the latter earning him an Oscar in addition. He features from time to time on the Facebook pages of his dog, Jango.

Perfect partners

Glyn Jones

Glyn and Osborne

I was a radar operator in the Royal Navy, but unfortunately I failed my medical for Dartmouth because of 'insensitive reflexes in my left leg,' and was medically retired. Ironically, with hindsight, I know that this is one of the earlier pre-cursors of multiple sclerosis (MS).

By 2006 I was wheelchair-dependent. I lived in a cottage out in the country, where I kept chickens, and had a huge garden with fruit trees. I also had a beautiful Alsation dog, Bud, who had been my only constant companion throughout the progression of my illness, including my move to sheltered accommodation.

We made the best of a bad job. We tried to settle but missed the freedom and space we had enjoyed previously. Apathy and depression set in. Then, when Bud got trouble in his hips, I just stayed in looking after him … until I had to let him go.

It is still the hardest decision I have ever had to make. He had been with me every second of my struggle. He had been there the nights I had cried myself to sleep. Now I was alone.

I sank into depression. I couldn't go out alone. My health deteriorated. My breathing got so bad I was given a ventilator, but I still had to get up for two hours in the middle of the night panicking about my breathing. You become even more scared when you're totally alone.

Thankfully, about the time that I was really grieving over Bud, a concerned friend persuaded me to contact Canine Partners, and just when I thought I could

© Jenny Moir/Canine Partners

get no lower, I got the call to the training centre at Heyshott! Things were moving.

Then Osborne happened, and suddenly there was hope. It was love at first sight. The training was excellent but hard emotionally, as well as physically.

I remember sitting in the taxi with Osborne waiting to come home. I realised that the whole of his life until now had been geared to this moment and how special he was; how lucky I was. Tears were shed.

Since then I have been reborn in stages. Now I have a new arm and legs in the form of Osborne. I will not fail Osborne, as he will not fail me. His needs and requirements are my priority; therefore I had to learn how to manage my fatigue around his timetable of needs!

Suddenly I find that being more active for him is making me fitter and healthier: my breathing problems disappear; my ulcers heal. He has improved my general health to the extent that I can now open my hand just stroking him.

The things he does for me save my energy for him. I laugh and cry every day – with happiness! From when I wake in the morning to when I go to bed, Osborne is there for me. He brings me his bowl for his breakfast, and brings the post to me. When my morning carer has me dressed, he assists me in the laundry room.

He opens the front door and off to the supermarket we go: when he takes my wallet up to the till to pay, the world stands still! We are well known, WELL LOVED figures now. People enjoy seeing our obvious bond. Our local supermarket checkout staff all but shout "pick me, pick me" as we approach, and I find reasons to go shopping now, rather than to avoid it.

Osborne picks up or tugs whatever I ask him, and does something new every day that makes me even happier. Osborne takes off my socks and trousers, and he can do my jacket, too, but we're still working on the shirt!

He is absolutely wonderful – almost intuitive! I owe him a huge debt: I am alive again. Osborne has brought me help, health; independence. He has renewed my faith in myself. He has given my life structure and purpose. Each day just gets better and better, and I intend to be the best partner in the world for him.

I promise that to myself every night as he tugs the quilt over my bare feet before he finally settles down to sleep himself … and I am not alone – EVER!

39

In the intervening years between being medically discharged from the Royal Navy and diagnosed with multiple sclerosis, Glyn did some security work for a couple of blue chip companies, and had five children, who have, so far, presented him with eight grandchildren.

As his health deteriorated, Glyn could no longer work. Now, he has only partial use of one arm and one hand, but Osborne is his other hand and legs.

Glyn cannot imagine what his life would be like without his canine partner.

Osborne was trained and provided by Canine Partners (see: www.caninepartners.org.uk).

Sammy and Sonny: darn fine dogs

David Belcher

Dog-wise, the Belcher clan has been doubly lucky: life has delivered us not one, but two darn fine dogs.

Belcher-wise, our two darn fine dogs have been the most even-tempered members of our family – the human components of which are, I must admit, prone to angst-ridden shouting, irrational rage, sulks and melodramatic self-pity. Over the past 20 years, our darn fine dogs have thus been a therapeutic boon, absorbing Belcherian rants and breakdowns with furry aplomb. Both our dogs have been non-stop radiators of adoration, unadulterated and non-judgemental, as well as guarantors of an enthusiastic, acrobatic welcome home: wet-nosed, warm-hearted somersaulting love-bombs ... with bad breath (hey, we all have our flaws).

Our first dog was a giant-eared, mouse-bodied Alsatian-hued terrier named Sammy, whom we found tied to a lamppost as an abandoned puppy. Throughout her life, Sammy remained endearingly grateful that we'd given her a home. She always seemed worried and slightly apologetic, as if fearing she'd be abandoned again if she did something wrong. Which she never did.

Our current dog is another 24-carat-gold cross-breed. Sonny arrived from a dog rescue centre as a wild-eyed and panic-stricken slobberer, before settling down and proving to be a pleasingly placid layabout. He still slobbers, mind you, which is just about the only thing he does wrong.

Neither of our dogs was or is perfect, of course. Neither has been especially receptive to training, ignoring all commands to cease and desist from chasing cats, foxes and/or squirrels.

Much more importantly, however, they've both been undemanding, uncomplaining, and evidently delighted to be wherever we are.

For 13 years, Sammy was our daughters' playmate, confidante and occasional dress-up doll (a small dog stuffed into a Partick Thistle football shirt is a winning addition to any social gathering).

For the past four years, Sonny has been a compliant lump, a willing stooge (a medium-sized dog squeezed into a novelty canine Santa Claus outfit makes a memorable if irreligious Christmas card).

Just as dogs provide entertainment, so dog ownership confers multiple health benefits. Daily dog walking promotes physical fitness. It also engenders mental wellbeing, as the business of emptying a dog can only be conducted at a calm,

My Dog, my Friend

David and Sonny

reflective pace dictated by the organic processes of nature. Oh yeah, filling poo-bags gives you bags of time to think.

Sure, dog ownership does have some malodorous downsides (perfumed poo-bags don't work). More particularly, Sammy never smelt of roses, which in part explains why we interred her cremated ashes beneath a rose bush.

As for Sonny, he eats grass to make himself sick on a semi-regular basis, thereby expunging the fur clogging his guts from his obsessive paw-licking habit. Bile, grass, fur: never a good look on a hall rug.

Take it from me, though: the best Belcher you'll ever meet has four legs and a waggy tail.

During 30 years of newsprint journalism, David Belcher helped slay many innocent trees. He is now a blameless radio broadcaster, northern soul DJ, and screenwriter. In his spare time he worries about Glasgow's most under-appreciated football club, Partick Thistle.

Flair of the dog

Ray Kelvin

Nestled on a nondescript road in an unremarkable part of north-west London, The Ugly Brown Building appears to be just another ordinary HQ. Venture inside, however, and you'll discover that not everything is as it seems.

To all intents and purposes, Winston is just a regular dog. He has four legs, a tail, two ears and a coat of fur, in a rather splendid colourway of mocha and mahogany, I might add. But anyone who has stepped into the fold at Tedquarters will tell you that he is *anything* but an ordinary guard dog.

For starters, how many hounds do you know that manage to pull off Bob Dylan's furrowed lines better than the man himself? Come to think of it, his rendition of 'If Dogs Run Free' is pitch perfect, too … not to mention that familiar brooding stare. Anyway, I digress.

While his home is in London, Winston guards the metaphorical keys to each of Ted Baker's many stores around the globe, and keeps them meticulously organised – in a crystal-embellished telephone box (naturally).

If rumours are to be believed, he also knows the face of every member of Ted Baker's wonderful team, and gives everyone a 'good day' nod as they enter in the morning. It's hungry work, I'm sure you'll agree, but Winston won't stop for breakfast until all 357 faces are welcomed (he gets a little cantankerous with tardy Teds).

How he manages without his morning feast remains shrouded in mystery, as does the tale of how Winston came to guard The Ugly Brown Building. Legend has it that he was a gift to the Queen from the Mayor of Nauru, whose ill-informed translator confused the Great British Pound with a Great Basset Hound. Our underdog's arrival at the palace was said to have caused uproar amongst Ma'am's Corgis, but we were quick to offer him a home from home/kennel from kennel.

Now, he's a part of the (dog-chewed) furniture, raising a smile with everyone he greets – even on a Monday morning. Some say he is the fountain of all creativity in the office, and all agree that a Tedquarters without Winston would be remarkably less colourful. He is, in all senses of the word, Ted Baker's top dog.

It's even said that the perfectly turned out security guards who keep vigil here were chosen to co-ordinate precisely with his food bowl. After all, Ted Baker prides itself on meticulous attention to detail … right down to the very last bone.

My Dog, my Friend

43

Winston: Ted Baker's top dog

Professor Ray Kelvin CBE is Founder and CEO of Ted Baker PLC. Ted Baker was born in 1988 and Winston has been with him since the beginning.

Biff and Roxy in the Vale of Years

Simon Callow

Simon, Biff (left) and Roxy at home

Biff and Roxy, Boxer twins, arrived from Wales late at night in the bleakest of winters. They were eight weeks old, and each fitted easily into a jacket pocket. They needed to pee, of course, and slid about in the icy garden, Biffy managing to plunge into the nearly frozen fountain, which terrified both him and us. He was towelled down and warmed up with various hot water bottles, which bred in him an early taste for being coddled.

The house, which was on three floors, had been fitted with gates and all sorts of devices to prevent the twins from plunging to their deaths. They mastered the deep stairs with astonishing speed, sometimes simply slithering down, seeming to enjoy the improvised slalom. They took to house training brilliantly, and the absorbent pads were soon abandoned.

Their characters quickly declared themselves: Roxy, nervous but feisty and curious, with an insatiable passion for stuffed toys, which she would shake to their deaths; Biffy, noisy but dreamy, given to long sessions staring at radiators, pondering the great questions of the universe. Their downy floppiness very quickly gave way to Boxer slim-waisted sturdiness, their faces settling, in his case into an expression of baffled nobility,

© Amy Clarke

in hers one of twinkling edginess. Roxy attached herself to my partner, Dan, Biffy to me, but above all they adored each other from the first day we saw them to the present.

They're ten years old now; Biffy has embarked on some sort of second youth, bouncy and needy, always emotional, always eager, while Roxy – whose eyesight and hearing have become somewhat impaired – has retreated into herself, which makes her seem much the older of the two. But their love of each other, their symbiotic closeness, is stronger than ever, and when we go for a walk on Hampstead Heath they chase each other furiously, pretending to snarl and snap. I live in dread of one predeceasing the other; just ten minutes out of each other's company is a misery to them.

Their essential good-nature and playfulness has been a central part of my life, and it is almost unimaginable that either, let alone both of them, should no longer define the meaning of home for me.

Simon Callow was born in London in 1949. He lived in Africa from 1958 to 1961, and it was here that he had his first dog, Judy, a Dalmatian/Bull Terrier cross. Many years passed doglessly, until 1984, when Brungie the Boxer entered his life. After Brungie came Merlie, a Lurcher, who, one terrible day, tore himself off the leash during his morning walk across Hampstead Heath, demonically impelled to chase a squirrel he'd spotted out of the corner of his eye across a major road, with tragic results. Merlie was followed by Basil, also a Lurcher, who died in harness ancient and rather noble. Biff and Roxy are his present companions. All the while, Simon was acting in films and plays, directing films and plays, and writing 13 books.

My constant friends

Fidelma Cook

At some point in the night, during my often-troubled sleep, I semi-wake to the gentle pressure of a body settling beside me; a back to my back.

Automatically I reach out a hand and stroke the silky hair of my silent companion, and return to a deeper, gentler, safer haven. All nightmares banished; all nocturnal fears irrational once more.

Come the morning I look at my anorexic, often neurotic Afghan and laugh at the fantasy that somehow she is the wolf-dog who will protect me, come what may, in my remote French home.

Most times she creates my worries – peering out through dark shuttered doors, a low aggressive growl in her throat. She frequently ballet-skips to imagined noises and threats leaving me fearful as to what she hears; my imagination running horribly, darkly, free.

As she disappears to the edge of my parc I have to face my own terrors to step into the night and beg her to return.

Yet when she pads through my always-open bedroom door and stretches her long body, head on pillow, next to mine, I know all is well.

I am not alone.

Portia is my fourth Afghan Hound, but only the latest, possibly the last, of so many dogs who have walked through my life and my heart.

Sally, a black Cocker Spaniel, was my first – a present from my grandfather when I was four years old.

Together we experienced snow for the very first time. Rare then in Ireland, my mother took us both out at two in the morning to tumble in the strange, wet whiteness that would be gone before daybreak.

Sally patiently allowed me to dress her up and wheel her around in a pram after I'd ditched the 'dead' dolls that held no appeal.

Like all my dogs to come, she was allowed into my bed, her hot breath in comforting rhythm with mine. Thankfully, I don't remember her death, only her.

Strange, her face is as clear to me now almost sixty years on as it was then.

Over the years the names and faces of my dogs have, as have those of people, faded from memory, although sometimes a face and a moment will return at the oddest time.

I think that is our dogs' unknowing gift. They depart far too quickly so allow us to put another in their place. Something we don't do with people. Well, maybe not quite so soon.

So, another dog arrives, whose trusting face soon replaces and morphs into the beloved one who has gone.

When I look at Portia, I see all her predecessors – Yana, Sukki, Tiggy – that same direct eye, same exquisite curve of the neck; detached, aristocratic pride. That is, of course, because of the breed.

But I remember them individually, too, by their idiosyncrasies – Suki with her phantom pregnancies, tenderly cradling her teddy bear baby; Tiggy a brindle sprite dead at seven; Yana, my first Afghan, the sweetest, gentlest dog rescued from unimaginable squalor without a stain on her character.

But I remember also my Airedales - not mine by choice – and their shocking aggression.

One, Rusty, brought to the city from the country, I took to walking back lanes in the early hours to avoid other dogs.

All my strength was needed to hold him back from attack. But at night he would position himself against my legs and hold up a paw in sorrow and entreat me to understand him.

And I will always remember the morning he admitted it was time, and my city vet arrived to send him into the most perfect last sleep.

I remember, too, Ben, the Labrador I 'sold' with our Scottish country house, who haunts me still as he howled and scratched the window as I drove away.

How do you tell a dog that his people have split up and there is no life for a free spirit in a city flat?

And I remember a flea-lice-ridden ugly mongrel found when I was 12 and loved passionately for a week before his owners claimed him back.

I recall leaning out of my bedroom window as the hand-over went on downstairs, and I couldn't say goodbye as I wept uncontrollably.

Strange the ones you remember.

Portia has my heart now. She's been with me more than any other dog.

We came to France together after I was made redundant from my newspaper.

Our first night was in a dismal, shabby flat as I waited for the keys of the house I'd bought, and sobbed and sobbed, thinking I had made the greatest mistake of my life.

In our overnight bags lugged from the car were all the pills and potions she needed, being a very sensitive, expensive dog.

© Patrick Durand

Fidelma and Portia

I'd had to buy some nameless, cheap food in the local market and offered it to her, expecting rejection. She wolfed it down and threw herself on the thin sofa bed with a deep sigh of contentment.

Meanwhile, I kept crying and wailing to all back home until, eyes red and swollen, I crawled into the bed in the cold, damp room.

Never in all of my life had I felt so low, so lost. I was shocked at my seeming despair.

As I shuddered in my misery, I heard the click of nails on the floor.

With a leap, a soft touch on my bed, Portia slipped in beside me, back into back.

I was not alone.

47

Fidelma Cook: journalist, author of French Leave, *columnist for the* Herald Magazine. *Freelancing from a field somewhere in La France Profonde. Cabin fever allayed by Portia - Thelma to her Louise.*

My lucky stars

Clare Allan

I wouldn't advise anyone to do it, but sometimes these things just happen. One New Year's Eve, a few years ago, I went to the park with one dog and came home with two.

It was a horrible day, dank and drizzly. Head down, hunched against the cold, I never even noticed the man until he seemed to appear quite suddenly, standing across my path. "I'll give you £100," he said. "If you'll take this bloody animal and keep her." In his hand was a lead and attached to the lead was the closest thing I've ever seen to misery in canine form. She was trembling, ears pressed flat to her head, a long, skinny body, crouched low to the ground, and at the far end a tragic stump of a tail. She'd been brutalised; that much was obvious, but there was something about her, a certain defiance, a flicker of spirit that refused to go out. The man began to list her transgressions, reeling them off like a criminal charge sheet. I caught her eye and the stump of a tail started barely perceptibly to quiver.

"Stop," I said. "Keep your money. I'll take her." He gave me the lead, and so began the most demanding, stress-inducing, labour-intensive, exasperating and deeply rewarding relationship of my life.

They say dogs are good for mental health, and undoubtedly they can be. My first dog, Billie, I got after being sectioned, and she effectively served as a mental health guide dog, leading me back out into the world and quite possibly saving my life. Dogs provide structure and routine, social contact, acceptance, affection; you'd be hard put to design a care plan more conducive to mental wellbeing. Dogs are good for mental health, *in general*, but it must be said, in those first few months Meg was very bad for mine.

I have never encountered anyone with Meg's capacity to get into trouble. Whether this stems from her early experience, her genes or my own ineptitude (I suspect an element of all three), within the space of six months she had had me arrested, been rescued by the fire brigade, knocked a child off his scooter, locked herself in the car (it took the AA to get her out), and leapt in a raging, flooded river, out the far side and over a wall to round up a flock of pregnant sheep and park them by the farmhouse.

A more cunning and curious, agile, athletic, tenacious and downright exhausting creature it is difficult to imagine. Not that she meant any harm, of course. The most heartbreaking thing was how badly she wanted to be loved. Indeed, it was often this very desire that got her into trouble. If a passer-by so much as smiled vaguely in Meg's direction, she would hurl herself at them joyfully. One morning I was chatting to a neighbour at her door, when Meg snuck past her into the house, raced up the stairs, and climbed into bed with her somewhat startled husband.

We saw four different trainers. My library of dog books, already substantial, trebled in size. Everyone knew what I needed to do, but nobody agreed with anyone else. She needed less exercise, one woman said; she was overstimulated. She needed to mix with sheep, said another, so I took her to a farm and she mixed with sheep, special dog-resistant sheep. "They won't run," they said. "You can let her off." So I let her off. They did.

In the end what Meg needed was time and patience, lots and lots of patience. I'm not a particularly patient person but getting annoyed with Meg was pointless: she simply blanked it out. And if she asked for patience, she showed it, too. We both made plenty of mistakes but neither of us ever gave up, and gradually the trust between us grew. Until, one day, I realised a week had gone by since she'd done anything truly awful. And then a month, then several months (it does depend a little, of course, on how you define 'truly awful.' Thankfully, I've learned to be flexible).

Clare and Meg

I wouldn't advise anyone to do it, but have I ever regretted the decision I made that New Year's Eve in the park? God, yes! Dozens of times! But not a fraction of the number that I've thanked my lucky stars – the strange constellation that brought us together, and gifted me this remarkable dog who has driven me to utter distraction and filled me with unabashed joy.

49

Clare Allan is the author of Poppy Shakespeare. *Her second novel,* Everything Is Full of Dogs, *will be published in 2014. She writes for* The Guardian *on mental health, and lives with two dogs, a Staff called Elsie, and a dog of indeterminate heritage called, amongst other things, Meg.*

Daisy the dog

Richard Holloway

Daisy the dog
6 Blantyre
Terrace
Edinburgh
EH10 5AE

Lorna Beckett
London N16

Dear Lorna,

You've asked me how I spend my days, so I thought I'd send you a letter to explain how busy I am. I hope you don't think it's too boring.

Papa usually wakes early, about 7 most mornings, sometimes earlier than that. I usually ignore him at first, though I look at him with one eye as he passes my bed to go into the bathroom. Sometimes the noise of the shower really wakes me, so I get up and nose my way into the bathroom to let him know I'm up. If he is standing there drying himself I help him by giving his legs a good licking, which saves him having to rub them with the towel. By the time he is dressed I am waiting for him at the door to go for the papers – though, if it's one of those really dark, cold, windy Edinburgh mornings, I sometimes just stay in bed and let him get the papers himself. I like that first walk of the day, though it's not really a walk, and Papa doesn't let me spend too much time smelling walls and lampposts, which is a pity, because those early morning smells are particularly delicious and informative.

Back home in the kitchen, Papa reads his paper and Gramma reads hers, as they have breakfast. Papa does not like to talk at breakfast, which is why he is always a bit edgy when people are visiting, because they usually think it's alright to talk, not realising that Papa can't read his paper and talk at the same time, and it's the paper he prefers. His way round this is to get up early when there are guests around so that he can have a quiet breakfast with the paper before they come into the kitchen. Gramma shakes her head at this and says he's para-something or other, a word I don't know, but I think it means mad.

Richard and Daisy

After breakfast, if he is not out at meetings, Papa goes into his study. Sometimes I join him and catch up on my sleep, since dogs need much more sleep than humans, but I usually have to do my own work first. I have two duties: one at the back of the house, looking out at the garden; one at the front of the house, looking out at the street. My duty at the back of the house is to watch out for Jo Jo, the overweight black cat from number 10, and warn Fred when she appears. Fred is the fat brown fieldmouse who lives under the little hut in the corner of the garden. He lives off the seeds that fall from Gramma's bird feeder, and he is fat because lots of seeds fall from the feeder, birds being such messy eaters. Cats don't like mice, though I can't figure out what they have against them, because there's no way a little mouse could be a problem for a cat, which is much bigger.

My Dog, my Friend

Maybe there's a cruel streak in them. Whatever the reason, I know that Jo Jo tries her best to catch Fred, which is where I come in. I lie on the back of the little sofa in Gramma's study, which looks out on the garden, and keep my eyes fixed on the back wall. If I see an ugly black blob appearing on the wall I bark loudly, which is my signal to Fred to get back under the hut. So far I have been successful at keeping him safe. That pretty well takes care of the morning, with the odd nap thrown in, because constant guard duty can be quite tiring.

My afternoon duty is much more fun. That's when I stand on the red armchair that Papa has placed in the window of the sitting room upstairs, so that I can keep an eye on the street and greet passers-by. Blantyre Terrace is known as the friendliest street in Edinburgh because I am there at the window of Number 6 to greet people. I spend a lot of time wagging my tail, which is what I do when I am happy. And I am at my happiest when people go past my window. I give the person who brings the letters in a big bag a particular welcome. The one I really like best, however, is Nikki, who lives across from us. When she comes out of her door I wag my tail so fast the human eye is not able to detect it. She normally waves at me and sometimes blows me a kiss, though Papa says these are really for him, since dogs don't kiss but humans do.

The really anxious time for me is later in the afternoon. This is the time when I expect to go for a long walk outside. Most days it happens, but some days it doesn't, for no apparent reason, which is very upsetting. That is why from about 3 o'clock onward I keep a firm eye on Papa, if he's in, or Gramma if he's out, to make sure they haven't forgotten that it is time for what they call Walkies. Most days it happens, to my great delight. The word is said and I go mad with joy at the prospect of getting out to savour all the smells of the outside world. There are about four different types of walk. There is the street walk, which varies in length, though it is usually about thirty minutes long. Then there is the walk across Bruntsfield Links into the Meadows. Then there is the Craighouse Hill walk, a full hour, much of it in a wood. But the really monstrous walk is in the Pentland Hills. I love those giant walks, but I have to confess that when they are over I curl up and sleep for hours.

You can see, therefore, what a busy life I lead. I know you are busy too, with school, with helping to look after Gillie, and with playing games. One more thing: what I like most of all when I am at the sitting room window keeping an eye on the street is when a big, black taxi draws up outside Number 6, the doors open and out you and Gillie come with your mummy and daddy to pay us a visit. Please come again soon.

Love from,

Daisy

Richard Holloway, now a writer and broadcaster, is the former Bishop of Edinburgh and Primus of the Scottish Episcopal Church. His latest book is Leaving Alexandria: A memoir of faith and doubt. *Daisy is his third Border Terrier and current spiritual adviser.*

Little old Sam

Ben Rimalower

I just got back from spending Thanksgiving with my parents, but being home for the holiday wasn't the same without Sammy. Sammy was part Chow, part Golden Retriever, so right through old age, he resembled an adorable puppy that you just wanted to snuggle. But on the inside, Sammy was a surly old man who did not enjoy being cuddled and cooed over.

A born hunter, Sammy's passion was chasing squirrels around the backyard – an avocation for which he had limitless energy and patience. In the ten

Sammy liked holidays when our family was together

© George Rimalower

years he lived with my family, I would guesstimate he spent about 30,000 hours in pursuit, only to catch like, what, five tree rats and a possum? He never lost heart, though.

Anyone who came to our house was an intruder, potentially interfering with his life's work, and was greeted with hostility.

But for my family, Sammy had warmth. When the five of us would sit together on the sofa in the den watching a movie, Sammy would come in through the doggie door (invigorated after a hunting expedition, albeit doubtlessly a failed one), and do what my family came to call a 'drive-by.'

Immediately, we'd call, "Sammy!" "Hi, Puppy!" We'd reach out our arms, "Here, Sammy." "Come here, boy."

No one expected Sammy to jump on the couch and nestle or even curl up at our feet; we all knew he was headed for his spot on the satisfyingly cold marble floor, but he always took the long way, around the square coffee table along the inside perimeter of the couch, allowing each of us to graze him with affection. We knew we were special.

I knew I was special when I'd get to the house after months away and Sammy would squeak and squeal with excitement

53

My Dog, my Friend

at seeing me. Moments later, he'd return to his routine, but I felt the love.

And I felt the love when my parents were out of town and Sammy and I stayed alone in the house. A smoke alarm beeped in the middle of the night for battery replacement, and there was Sammy at the side of my bed, politely pawing my shoulder. He didn't want to trouble me, but he needed help.

It was no trouble at all.

Ben Rimalower is the writer and original star of Off-Off-Broadway's long-running hit solo play 'Patti Issues' (New York Times Critics Pick, Bistro Award, MAC Award), which he continues to tour all over the world. He writes for Playbill *and the* Huffington Post. *In addition to directing a number of plays Off-Broadway, Ben was called "the Midas of Cabaret" by* The Advocate *for helming a slew of solo shows, most notably conceiving and directing 'Leslie Kritzer is Patti Lupone at Les Mouches.' Follow @benrimalower on Twitter and visit benrimalower.com.*

Pets As Therapy - READ2DOGS programme

The value of the Pets As Therapy READ2DOGS programme is in its simplicity. Many children will feel naturally comfortable in the presence of dogs; they may often have pet dogs at home. Parents and teachers can use this special relationship to enhance literacy skills and encourage reading in a relaxed situation, with dog and child sitting together. This contact between dog and child encourages physical interaction, which helps to put the child at ease (contact with a friendly dog has been proven to lower blood pressure and reduce stress in many different types of situation).

READ2DOGS gives children the opportunity to practise and enjoy reading privately, away from their peers and to an audience that will enjoy the experience as much as they do.

Pets As Therapy has PAT dogs running READ2DOGS programmes around the UK. The feedback and reported improvement in participating children has been wholly positive. Teachers are reporting increased reading age scores; improved social skills; a reduction in behavioural issues, and better concentration levels.

More information is available at www.petsastherapy.org.

Aero - a Pets As Therapy dog participating in the READ2DOGS programme

Wesley and Aero enjoying time together in the READ2DOGS programme

My Dog, my Friend

The following extracts have been written by children* between the ages of eight and ten, who spend time reading with Aero –

Aero helped ~~that~~ me read because I wasn't embarrassed to read in front of ~~him~~ her and a small group. It was also relaxing to read while stroking her tail. I liked it when she lay there next to us and listened because it made us feel like we were being respected and that we were being listened to.

Lucy, aged nine

Aero

Aero made me feel confident with my reading and also she made me feel really happy with my reading and she made me feel like I was at home. I really enjoyed reading The Snow man She made me want to read all the time I never met a dog before Who's so inthuse astic.

Jamie, aged ten

Aero

At wootton every monday I was so extited to see a dog called Aero. We would read and some people would write whith her. She is brown, choclotte couler. Evryone liked her and she was a petacherape dog and she is a choclotta brown labrador. She is so cute. We wread litted red ridding hood. We would wread to her to bilud up are confidence on wreading. She is so cute and friendly. She is great!!!

Nina, aged nine

My Dog, my Friend

Aero (Erin)

Reading to Aero helped me build my confidence a bit and made me think I can read more than just my sort of age book but any thing

She's a very nice dog. She made me feel comfortable and warm inside. I remember it was yesterday she wagged her tail with Joy. She had a lovely soft coat and a nice chocolate colour. She's a lovely dog thank you for it!

Thank you!

Erin, aged nine

Aero (Anna)

Reading to Aero was exciting and she encouraged you to read out lowd. You would think that it is a bit wierd reading to a dog. When I read to Aero she wagged her tail. My favorit time was when we do a story about Aero and I did her being a super dog it was fun.

thank you for choosing me to read to you

Anna, aged nine

Aero (Max)

She made me feel happy and nice the way I stroaked her nice smooth body and reading goldie locks and the 3 bears she was realy enjoying it. And also I remember when she walked in to the door that was very funny. She helped me by making me feel at home and also how she helped me was by letting me no dogs are very very very very special to me and every body els. And I liked when we got to feed her special treats. I liked when she lied on her back so we could tickle her tummy she is the best labrodoor I have ever met in my live. I think my dog grace will like her they would play together forever.

What she looks like: Brown fur, browneyes, a waggy tail

Max, aged nine

Joe

Aero helped me to read because I used to be shy and a little bit scared but then as I carryed on reading I got better and better at reading and now im a free reeder and I was not scared of Aero because my nan has 2 dogs.

Joe, aged eight

Pup
Helen FitzGerald

As a child, I was stick-thin, cross-eyed, had a hole in my heart, and chronic asthma. The twelfth of thirteen children, I was the runt of the litter. Our house was crammed with noisy siblings vying for space, and not getting any. Our one acre garden was almost as busy with the animals Mum refused to name ("We should not impose human names on our wild ones," she'd say). So mother cat, puss, puss, chook (x 25), budgie (x 13), duck, ferret and Pup also vied for space in our dry, rocky Aussie garden.

We lived on the edge of the small town of Kilmore: home to commuters, horse-racers, and Assumption College boarding school, a breeding ground for women-hating, Aussie rules footballers.

What I needed most as a child was my own space. I needed to get away from the boy bullies who chanted cruel nicknames as I scurried home from netball or the Milk Bar. "Bone face!" "Bjorn!" they'd chant. Back home, I'd want to hide somewhere and cry, mortified at my thin face, at my boyish frame, at my unfortunate post-perm Bjorn Borg hairstyle.

But there was nowhere to hide at home.

Pup was my escape.

My sister won him on the spinning

wheel at the Assumption College fete. She carried him across the disused railway, past the old jail where Ned Kelly's father apparently engineered a daring escape, past the bacon factory and the sale yards, to our seventies brick house. As with all unwanted animals, Mum welcomed him, and refused to impose a name on him. We were told he was a cross between a Labrador and a Poodle, but now that Labradoodles are everywhere, I know he was no such thing. With unruly wavy brown hair that he refused to let us clip, he was as scruffy and undesirable as I was.

In the evening, I'd walk Pup to the end of our street, past the Church of England to the dirt road we called the 'back lane.' My school friends never went there. Assumption boys never went there. I don't remember ever meeting a single soul on that track. I'd take off Pup's lead and watch him run across the field until he reached the dam. He'd hurl himself in, and, after a swim, follow me all the way to the Ostrich farm on the hill. Hot and tired, he'd sniff the surrounds happily as I lay on the ground and shut my eyes.

I can smell that moment now: dry grass, eucalyptus.

I can hear it: Pup's happy panting. No Assumption boys. No siblings. Ah …

Helen FitzGerald writes thrillers and teen fiction. She's been described as "a startling new talent in the edgier corner of the crime fiction scene." Her novels have been translated into numerous languages, and widely praised as "glorious black comedy" and "thinking women's noir." Website: www.helenfitzgerald.net; follow Helen on twitter: @fitzhelen

Why are you not out walking with me more?

Nanette Mutrie

If dogs could speak they would say to us "Why are you not walking with me more?"

Every time I start making preparations to go out the house my dog, Ellie, sits behind the door always ready for another walk. We probably know dogs need to walk but maybe we know less about our own need to be active?

Walking has been described as the nearest thing to perfect exercise – wow! That is important because being physically active is one of the best things we can do for our health. We already know that physical activity levels are higher for adults who own dogs than those who don't. This may not be surprising to you since dogs demand to be taken out for toileting, and most dogs love to play or go for long walks. For owners, this level of physical activity becomes routine since these demands are, of course, made by dogs at least two or three times in the day. This is a huge benefit for the person walking the dog who is now being active in a habitual way and on a daily basis, without thinking too hard about "when can I fit some activity in for myself today?"

Walking has been described as 'almost perfect exercise' but many people might ask "Is walking really enough?" However, there is plenty of evidence that this routine level of physical activity will have substantial physical and mental health benefits – see the Toronto Charter for Physical Activity if you need to be convinced.

These health benefits are perhaps under-emphasised within a fitness industry that wants us to join the gym, go to supervised classes or use a personal trainer ... because they cannot make money from us achieving our physical activity goals by simply walking the dog! There's a great social health benefit, too: I know all my neighbours by their dog's name, and the walking-the-dog habit might just rub off on other friends or family members as different people may join your walks at different times.

So if your dog seems to be saying to you "Why are you not out walking with me more?" be glad that he or she demands to be taken out for a walk, and perhaps even consider an extra walk today or a longer route tomorrow! That tail will be wagging for sure if you do.

And if you don't have a dog at the moment ... take it for a walk anyway!

My Dog, my Friend

Nanette with Jock – her first of three Border Terriers, fondly remembered by young Ellie

Nanette Mutrie is Professor of Physical Activity for Health at the University of Edinburgh, Scotland. With her students and colleagues, she has published over 200 journal articles on exercise, including how to increase the amount of exercise that people take, and the positive effects of exercise on health and wellbeing. Nanette is frequently taken for a walk by her dog, Ellie.

Harvey, prison, and me

A young offender

2011 couldn't have started any worse for me. I'd been given a lengthy prison sentence just days before my twentieth birthday. I can remember thinking that already my life was over.

I was sent to Polmont Young Offenders Institution, where, to my amazement, I heard that there was a dog training course starting soon. Although I had no experience in dog training, I'd always loved animals, so I decided to volunteer for the course.

My first day on the dog training course couldn't have gone any better. I was given a great little dog called Ollie to work with. Our teacher, Rebecca, was amazing, and I managed to keep out of trouble for a few hours – a first for me.

After the training finished, I went back to my cell, and for the first time since coming to prison I felt happy and couldn't wait for the next session.

Once my first eight weeks were up, Rebecca asked me if I would like to stay on the course as a peer mentor, which basically meant that I would have more responsibilities. Ollie had just been successfully rehomed after 18 months with Dogs Trust, and Rebecca told me that she had a more challenging dog at the rehoming centre that she would like me to work with.

I was over the moon at the chance, and of course said yes.

That's when I met HARVEY!

Harvey was a big Staffy-cross, and, like Ollie, had been with Dogs Trust for a long time. I don't think Harvey had been trained to do hardly anything before, so I knew I had my work cut out with this one.

At the start of our training sessions we would always begin by taking the dogs for a walk around the grounds, although I'm sure it was Harvey taking me for a walk in our first few sessions together. Then we'd go round to our outdoor training area where Harvey loved to play 'tug' and 'fetch' with his rope toy, and practise agility training. Harvey was surprisingly good at the trotting poles: honestly, for a dog the size of a body builder, he had the grace of a ballerina.

My favourite part of the session was the one-to-one training we did indoors, where each of us had our own closed-off area. This is where I taught Harvey many of the skills to help him pass his APDT (Association of Pet Dog Trainers) Good Companion Award. Harvey made such brilliant progress that he actually became the first dog on the course to pass the award with full marks, something I am very proud of.

On the days that Harvey wasn't

My Dog, my Friend

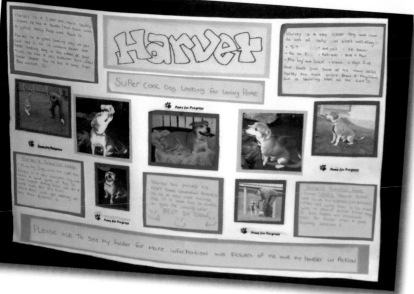

Paws for Progress is a collaborative project between the Scottish Prison Service, Dogs Trust, and the University of Stirling, and is the only prison-based dog training programme in the UK. It aims to improve the behaviour, education and employability prospects of the young men involved, and improve the behaviour, wellbeing and rehoming prospects of the dogs. See: www.pawsforprogress.com.

there, I would update his training diary, prepare his training plans, and make posters about him. All of this would go to the rehoming centre so that anyone visiting the centre could look at it.

Just a week before I turned 21 and was due to move to an adult prison, Harvey was successfully rehomed. As much as I would miss him, I was really pleased for him as he was a great dog who deserved a good home, and to think I helped him in some way makes it that little bit more special.

Paws for Progress did so much for me in such a short time. Before I started the course I was constantly getting into trouble, and my behaviour was something that I wanted and needed to change. I think that seeing how Harvey changed his so easily helped me to change mine, as since my first day on the course I've not been in any trouble.

I also think that making the material to help promote Harvey for rehoming changed how I felt about learning and writing. Although I'm in a different prison now and can no longer train dogs, I still write essays for Paws for Progress, and I have started education classes in creative writing, English and art, and I'm working towards my Higher English, too.

When I'm released, I hope I can use the skills I've gained through Paws for Progress to get a job working with dogs, and I hope that one day I can help more dogs like Harvey have better futures.

So thank you, Paws for Progress, Rebecca and Harvey, for having a huge impact on helping me change my life for the better.

Love cured me

David Shrigley

I didn't used to like dogs. I grew up with a cat but when I left home, after a few years I developed an allergy to them. I seemed to be even more allergic to dogs.

Then my wife decided we should get a dog. I said it was not a good idea because I might die of an asthma attack. My wife said we would get a non-shedder. I said I still might die of an asthma attack. My wife said not to be so melodramatic.

She kept on about the dog. We don't have any kids and I guess we had an emotional gap to fill, so eventually I said yes to the dog. As long as it was small. And a non-shedder.

On 1st September 2012 my wife drove from Glasgow to Essex to fetch a black Miniature Schnauzer. She let me name her. I chose the name Inka because she was black. Like ink.

Anyway, when Inka arrived I did a bit of a '180' on dogs. Not only did I fall in love with Inka but I decided that I now liked ALL dogs.

Two weeks later I had my first asthma attack. I guess it took a while maybe because Inka is a non-shedder. But I persevered with antihistamine and an inhaler, and after about three or four months I was okay. Now I don't need the anti-histamine and I rarely need the inhaler.

I think it was love that cured me.

Life has changed quite a lot since we got Inka. I have to get up early and take her for walks, and we don't go on foreign holidays anymore. She has made us happy, though.

Life is better with Inka.

What I like most about dogs is that their needs are very few. If you feed them and play with them and take them out then they are happy. But essentially they just need you.

My wife and I refer to our new family unit as 'the pack.' My wife is pack leader and Inka and I vie to be second-in-command.

David with Inka on the day she arrived

David Shrigley is one of the tallest artists currently working in Scotland. He has exhibited his drawings, photographs and sculptures in galleries and museums worldwide. He is the author of many books of drawings, and has written and directed numerous animated films. He lives and works in Glasgow. www.davidshrigley.com

The Max Factor

Matthew Offord

My dog is called Max. Actually, his full name is Maximus Decimus Meridius and he is named after the main character in the film *Gladiator*. The name suits him because he is a Jack Russell terrier and is absolutely fearless. He is relatively small, and is white-and-tan coloured. When we first met Max, his brother and two sisters fell over each other to be introduced to us, and he jumped up on my lap to lick my face. I like to think that he chose us instead of the other way around.

My wife and I decided to get a dog after we got married. Having been elected to Parliament, I felt that Max could accompany me in my activities, and also stay with me in my office in Westminster. Several years ago I met with a senior officer in a council, whose dog sat both contentedly and quietly in a bed beneath a desk: I had a view that my dog would do the same.

The day after Max came home with us he accompanied me into work, and very quickly settled into his routine. He likes to have a sleep in the morning, but will get up to see who enters the office, though after a quick sniff will often go back to bed. Sometimes he chews rawhide but he also likes to take papers and envelopes out of the bin and tear them up, leaving a paper trail behind him.

When I open the door of the office he will accompany me to other offices, and also knows the way to my office staff. In their room he knows where they keep the treats, and will sit on his hind legs asking for a chew. On the way out of the office he will, without fail, inspect their bin to see who had what for lunch.

Max is not just a visitor to others but also hosts guests himself. One MP brings his children to my office to see Max; a member of the House of Lords brings his dog for meetings, and a police officer and member of the House of Parliament security team brings him dog treats.

One accolade that has eluded us thus far is winning Westminster Parliamentary Dog of the Year. Max's first entry saw him placed third, but last year, even though he appeared on the BBC's *Breakfast News* on the morning of the competition, we were not placed. So expectation remains high for the next event (held each October), and we are keeping our paws crossed that it will be third time lucky.

Max makes a regular appearance on the Underground, and I remember the first time he travelled by tube train. Contained in a small bag, his head poking over the top, he watched people as they cooed over him, and it was not long before he was out of the bag and sitting at our feet. Other passengers tell me how amazed they are that he sits so quietly, while I often catch others watching him with a smile on their faces. Sometimes they ask if they can stroke him, and it's not unusual for people to take pictures on their mobile phones – one even asked to have their picture taken with him! Max seems to like the tube as he gets to meet so many people and several of the staff – and newspaper vendors at the stations know him by name. Sometimes, he is lucky enough to see another dog commuter, and passengers in the carriage laugh when he squeaks if he cannot get near enough to say hello.

How would I describe my relationship with Max? We probably spend more time with each other than we do with anyone else – including my wife – so I would claim that we are close. He trusts me and allows me to touch his mouth, his ears and his feet, or anywhere else that he won't allow the vet to! He runs to me and jumps into my arms when he is scared, and I turn to him when I am anxious or worried. I find it helps to stroke him while I consider political problems or constituent issues.

Max is a good ice-breaker when I meet people for the first time. People who have dogs will tell me about them, while people who don't make a fuss of Max as he is a novelty to them. Even when he is not with me constituents often ask after his welfare or where he is.

Max is very special to me. He is the confidant who never reveals secrets; the friend who never betrays; the companion who never complains, and the defender who always protects. But most of all, he is my dog, Max.

© Claire Offord

Westminster Dog of the Year in 2011, in which Max was placed third

67

Matthew Offord is the Conservative Member of Parliament for Hendon. Prior to his election in 2010, Matthew was Deputy Leader of Barnet Council, and he worked for the BBC as a political adviser.

Matthew lives in Hendon with his wife, Claire, and dog, Max, who keeps him company in his Westminster office.

A 'really clever' dog

Stanley Coren

Dogs are certainly intelligent when compared to other animals. In fact, psychologists have shown that the mental ability of a dog is nearly the same as a human being aged between two and three years. Sometimes, however, humans overestimate the cleverness of dogs and their ability to be trained simply because we interpret their behavior from our own point of view, and believe that everything that they do must have a meaning and a purpose. I encountered an example of this when I was hosting a fund raising event for a shelter in New Brunswick.

We had arranged for a number of 'acts,' including a dog that herded ducks, one that did scent discrimination, others that performed agility tricks, some that jumped very high, and even a pair of dogs that danced with their masters. For comic relief we had Rupert, a loveable, lop-eared Basset Hound.

An hour or so prior to the event I easily taught Rupert that food treats might be found in several places around the stage. Later, at unpredictable times, Rupert would be released during another act. He would simply appear randomly from one side or another of the stage and wander around leisurely, seemingly aimlessly, but really searching for the food that he believed must be hidden someplace on or around the stage. This served as the opportunity for some funny banter about how Rupert was 'interfering with the normal progress of the show,' and how Basset Hounds 'are dogs with their own agenda which might never be understood by humans.' Rupert came across as a lovable but perhaps dopey dog, and my running commentary about him and his behavior made the audience chuckle and kept the mood light.

At one point during the proceedings, while a Labrador Retriever was demonstrating how he could catch three tennis balls in his mouth at once, Rupert sauntered across the stage once more. Having eaten quite a few treats by then, he stopped in the middle of the floor and relieved himself. The crowd roared with embarrassed laughter. Making the best of the situation I mock scolded him over the microphone "Now, Rupert! Stop that and act like a gentleman!" Apparently, Rupert's bottom itched from the previous activity, so he put his rear end down on the floor, and dragged it across the stage and out of sight using only his front legs. The crowd laughed wildly so I improvised: "Rupert, have you forgotten how to act politely?" at which moment he appeared again, going in the opposite direction, but still dragging his bottom across the stage. The auditorium collapsed in noisy giggles. Despite Rupert's indiscretion the audience clearly considered him to be one of the stars of the event.

After the show I was approached by two well known dog trainers who told me they had been quite impressed by the whole presentation. However, what they really wanted to know was how I had trained that "clever dog" Rupert to do "all that" ...

Stanley with Wizard, Dancer and Odin

© Lionel Trudel

Stanley Coren is Professor Emeritus in the Department of Psychology at the University of British Columbia. Although best known to the public for his books on dogs, he is also an award-winning behavioural researcher, a Fellow of the Royal Society of Canada, and was named as one of the 2000 outstanding scientists of the Twentieth Century. His many books include Born to Bark, Do Dogs Dream? *and* How Dogs Think. *He is also the winner of the Maxwell Medal of Excellence from The Dog Writers Association of America.*

A Son of Man's Best Friend

John Hegley

The Lord, I'm his sheepdog ... mind you,
you wouldn't have thought so
with all those disciples going 'Master this'
and 'Master, the other.'
He was MY Master, for goodness' sake.
I've got to say I didn't dig the way he sent
those pigs over the edge of that cliff,
but you just have to deal with your doubt
and stay loyal.
And it did feel a bit wrong him striding
the tide
with me behind, doggie paddling,
but we had a chuckle, even if he did
forget to put water in my bowl sometimes.
I liked that walk in the wilderness best!
Forty days and nights, just US.
No disciples. And no MULTITUDE.
THEY used to get my goat ... 'OOH, look
at all the loaves and fishes.'
... THEY never saw him lying in bed at
night, sweating about saving humanity.
I like to think stroking me did him some
good,
even if it was a bit absent-minded,
sometimes.
I hope the patter of my paws of a morning
was reassuring.

The disciples didn't seem to realise he
had doubts of his own.
When they all nodded off in the garden,
who was the one who stayed alert the
whole hour?
He only ever told me I was a bad dog that
once in the temple
when I bit the money-lenders.
But, he started it.
And when the Romans came for him, I
went for them, as well,
but they were armed to the eyeballs and
that was the end of me.

So, there I am, up in heaven looking out
for him.
He comes through the gate
and he says,
'I've felt incomplete without you.
I've hated us being apart.
But, I've always known you were there for
me.'
And I turn around
and he's talking to his dad!
I went over and licked his feet anyway,
though.
He likes that.

70

71

John Hegley is one of Britain's most popular contemporary poets. Dogs, handkerchiefs, glasses, miseries of human existence and root vegetables are recurring themes in his works, and it's been reported (in The Observer *newspaper) that "John is to potatoes what Wordsworth has been to daffodils."*

His many books include Uncut Confetti, Peace Love and Potatoes, The Sound of Paint Drying, My Dog is a Carrot *and* I am a Poetato.

Saturday, 30th May 2009 from Diary of a Dog-Walker

Edward Stourton

We are in Battersea Park, across the river from Chelsea, and one or two of the hacking jackets on display are cut with just a little more dash than is strictly necessary for dog-walking.

They are all there – the sniffers and trotters, the sprinters and plodders, the yappers and slobberers, the shaggy and the *soigné*. While they do their doggy thing about our feet, we, their masters and mistresses (or perhaps their servants?), do ours. We talk. Here, I have discussed everything from high politics in the Middle East to the low points of divorce, from children and jobs through plays, books and exhibitions to holiday homes, the credit crunch, and – of course – canine triumphs and tragedies. This easy-going social intercourse is the great revelation of dog-owning in the middle age. If you are accompanied by a dog you can talk to anyone, and anyone can talk to you – about anything.

To get there, you need the capacity for benign amnesia that allows mothers to repeat the pain of childbirth, and authors to submit themselves to the racking anxieties of a new book. I once shared my life with a rumbustious Spabrador (a Spaniel/Labrador cross), but even her most searing indiscretions have now been rose-tinted into jolly anecdotes. When she was a puppy my daughter trained her to use a sheet of newspaper

© Andrew Crowley

Edward and Kudo, the subject of his diary

as her lavatory: one Sunday morning she jumped on to the bed as I was reading the *Sunday Telegraph* and, before you could say 'Pavlov,' there it was, hot and steaming in the middle of a piece of finely crafted prose from Sir Peregrine Worsthorne (no offence, I am sure, intended).

You also need a post-modernist ability to hold two completely contradictory views simultaneously in your mind. We who make our regular pilgrimage to Battersea Park know that a dog is just a dog (whatever the park's splendid Buddhist Temple may hint to the contrary), that it will never write a great book or win a Nobel Prize. We know that evolution has taught it the charm that compels our attention to its wants and needs. And yet we allow ourselves to speak and think of dogs as friends, individuals with a full claim on our affections.

The reward is that dog-walking becomes like reading a novel, or watching a play: disbelief is suspended and, for an hour so, we are given license to escape ordinary life. Fantasy flourishes, and really quite trivial moments in dog life become a source of wonder to be repeated, discussed, laughed about and even worried over with its human family.

Edward Stourton is the author of six books. He is the writer and presenter of several high-profile current affairs programmes and documentaries for radio and television, and regularly presents BBC Radio Four programmes such as The World at One, The World This Weekend, Sunday *and* Analysis. *He is a frequent contributor to the* Today *programme, where, for ten years, he was one of the main presenters.*

Meeting the neighbours

Charlie Dimmock

Tarah (just for the record, not a name I would have chosen) is a very large, fluffy black Newfoundland I inherited from a friend, who - in turn - had taken her on at just over a year old as her original owners were going to have her put down because "they didn't realise that Newfoundland's got that big."

Before Tarah moved in I spent several weekends 'dog-proofing' the garden, which involved much stock fencing and many a curse as my fencing skills are not the best! But I got there and, with much excitement, went and collected my new five-year-old ball of fluff, who spent the next few days checking out the fencing and generally exploring the garden. (Note to self: Newfoundlands and ornamental ponds are not a good combination as Tarah seemed to believe the only way to drink from the pond was to fully immerse herself in it.)

On a positive note the fencing was doing fine ... until week two when one sunny afternoon my neighbour somewhat tetchily shouted over the hedge "Have you lost a dog?" With a quick glance round the garden and in the back door, I had to reply "um ... Yes, I think I have ..."

"It's in my lounge, eating my fruit and nuts", was the response.

"Oh ..."

Unfortunately, by the time I got into my neighbour's lounge there were very few fruit and nuts left, though much to my relief, it wasn't chocolate fruit and nut but the actual healthy stuff.

On the downside, after her little snack, much to my embarrassment, Tarah wanted to play chase round my neighbour's house, and although I apologised, fixed the hole in the fence, and replaced the snaffled fruit and nuts (with the luxury version), I don't think that Tarah endeared herself to my neighbour.

Thankfully, the neighbours on the other side absolutely love her.

Their grandson - who's frightened of dogs - was playing cars in their garden one day when Tarah wandered in and calmly sat down to watch him play, before giving him a sloppy lick on his face. The little lad carried on playing, his new friend - Tarah - looking on.

Some time later he ambled into the house to let his grandmother know that there was a "lost black bear in the garden." She pointed out that it wasn't a bear but actually a dog, and since then he's been much happier in the company of dogs, even helping to walk Tarah home that day.

My fence is now totally Tarah-proof and very robust ... however, one thing I've

© Adrian Houston

Charlie and Tarah

noticed is Tarah isn't as enthusiastic about visiting my fruit-and-nuts neighbour's garden – guess she's been there and done that!

Charlie Dimmock is a gardening expert specialising in aquatics. She first came to the public's attention in 1997 as one of the team presenting the BBC's gardening programme Ground Force, *which went on to run for ten series. This involvement led to many other projects on TV such as* Charlie's Garden Army, Cheer for Charlie, *and* River Walks.

Charlie has also worked for CBS in New York on The Early Show, *and more recently has appeared in the theatre production of* Calendar Girls.

Companion

Jackie Kay

Funny – I never thought I was a dog person until I had my first, and so far only, dog; now I am a dog person without a dog, I feel very strange indeed. Not completely myself.

When I had a dog, I met other new-to-the-dog people who would say, with a sense of wonder, "I didn't know how much they could give you," and I would constantly bump into the well established dog people, the ones whose lives can be measured by the dogs they have owned, who would say with confidence "I've always been a dog person. I couldn't be without one." And some would even take that to the extreme and say "I can imagine being without my husband easier than I can without my dog." (In Sam's case, she's now divorced, and the dog is well settled into her ex-husband's space in the bed.)

The other day I was in a local café, On the Corner in Beech Road, which used to welcome my dog and me. The café woman came up to me and said, "Where's your wee dog?" "She died," I said. And the woman said, "Oh no, but she was your companion." And I felt the tears well up, but I also liked that she had said it simply, baldly stating a fact. Are you a dog person? I wanted to ask her, but I didn't because I had a big lump in my throat.

So after the dog-less visit to our café, I walked through our park, which I had avoided for a good time after my dog died. I looked at the flowers that she would first sniff then pee on, and at the little red bins that I no longer had any post for, and at the other people, the still-dog people out with their dogs who looked at me with too much sympathy, because they could understand what it would be like, out walking with no dog. (Only animal people could possibly understand dog grief. To everyone else, it is a huge indulgence. When my dog died I was away on holiday in Arran with a friend who had lost his wife only two months earlier. I hid my upset from him; it seemed unseemly.) One gay man, who runs the grooming parlour (just for dogs) called Betty and Butch stopped and said quite earnestly, "Do you find people avoiding you? I was about to avoid you, but I thought, no, I'll come and ask you how you are? I was like that when my first dog died," he said. "Other dog walkers can't face it," and I stood nodding and he kept talking on and then he left with his dog padding after him.

The first thing in the morning and the last thing at night are all different in the dog-less life. You wake up and have no dog to let out or walk or feed, no dog to begin your joint day with. And last

Jackie with Dinky

thing at night, no dog to stargaze with, to wait for as you let her out into the night air one last time before the morning. Dogs can pick up your mood, make you laugh; seem to intuit what you're thinking. Once you know a dog there's so many different kinds of barks, like tones in conversation. And once you know a dog, you realize how much you can communicate barker to talker, body to body. It is all animal. Maybe that's what humans need, an animal that brings out the instinct in them, the good instinct.

My dog's favourite little trick was going out the back door, walking along the lane down the alley, and picking out her own house on the row of terraced houses on our street. I'd go to answer the thump on the door, and there she'd be stood on the doorstep, grinning. She thought it very funny. It took me the longest time to get used to the empty space in the hall where dog and basket would lie together like some kind of joint enterprise, the one seeming to grow out of the other; to get used to not knocking over the bowl of water in the kitchen; to get used to not saying Good Night to my dog, and even more embarrassing, it took me ages to feel safe in my own house,

My Dog, my Friend

to not feel dog-less and jumpy in the midnight hours. Only the dog people will admit it but having a dog keeps the howl at bay. And not having a dog is like going about the place with something essential, even, it begins to feel, some part of you, missing. Something missing. Something not walking with you: all at once you are unaccompanied on the road. The dog-less walks in the beautiful highlands by the river Rannoch in Ardtornish, or by the Bronte Falls near Haworth, or by the river Mersey and the meadows near my home, I still imagine through my old dog's eyes, which ones she would have loved, which ones she wouldn't have been keen on.

Time to get a new dog, finally, I think a year and a bit later, asking myself, rather bluntly, how many dogs I've got left in me. I'm fifty-two now and if I get a puppy and she lives till I'm 66, would I be then thinking of getting a new dog at 66? Or if I get a rescue dog that is already four or five, might I have two rescue dogs left in me? Bloody hell, the clock ticking is a dog's bark: I can mark out my life in dogs.

I am suddenly mortal. I've gone from not even thinking of myself as middle aged to measuring how many dogs life might yet offer me, and the terrible truth is just one, really. No! Should have started being a dog person a whole lot sooner.

Established dog people say that the best compliment you can pay your dog is to replace her right away. But I couldn't manage that. I didn't think my dog would have liked it; her ashes are still on the mantelpiece. I've no idea how long they will stay there for. (I've heard of people that ask to be buried with their dog's ashes, but I don't think I'll go for that.) Now, though, the trees are all bare, the ground's covered with rusty leaves and spring will come not long after Christmas, with the fresh promise of new crocuses. I'm sure my old dog would understand. She did seem to understand everything, and even at the vet's in Brodick, just before the final injection, she looked at me and then through me one last time, as if she completely understood that she was saying goodbye.

Jackie Kay writes fiction and poetry. Her most recent books are Red Dust Road *(winner of the Scottish Book Award) and* Fiere *(shortlisted for the Costa. She teaches at the University of Newcastle and is a fellow of the Royal Society of literature.*

In praise of dogs

Esther Rantzen

There are so many good, logical reasons to have a dog. When we are at our laziest, if the cold winds blow and a storm threatens, a sleepy cat will encourage us to curl up next to him beside the fire. But dogs are made of sterner stuff. A dog will insist on exercise; he will whine by the door, fetch a lead, and find a hundred ways to beg for a long, brisk walk in all weathers, at least twice a day.

Good for him – and equally good for us.

If feeling stressed after a long day at the office, or an argument with a parking warden, when you get home a rabbit will simply ignore you. Twitch with misery or frustration, and a hamster will pay not the slightest attention. But a dog will come and comfort us; sit on our feet so we have to bend down and stroke him, and that warm, heavy weight will miraculously lower our blood pressure and elicit a smile.

A dog will discourage burglars by barking when the doorbell rings or a stranger walks up the path. A guide dog will act as our eyes if we lose our sight, or alert us to the beep of a smoke alarm or ping of the microwave if we lose our hearing. So there are many logical reasons to have a dog.

But we dog-lovers know it's not actually a question of logic: it's about love.

Dogs read our minds, and become the friends we need. I remember watching my son playing with our Labrador, Arthur. It was like seeing two puppies teasing and wrestling with each other. They would pretend to snarl, turn tail as if in panic, then rush back to the mock-attack, and finally, exhausted, fall on top of each other panting until their energy returned and the wrestling began again. They had become brothers.

But they can be serious, too, and can become very protective when danger looms. My family was walking together in the New Forest with our mongrel, Millie, one beautiful autumn day; deep in conversation together as she happily explored gorse bushes beside the path. Millie disappeared back the way we had come, and we heard her barking in the distance. Suddenly, she came streaking back and overtook us, turning to stop and sit, looking straight into my eyes.

I remembered that Millie had used the same technique once before, when she had just given birth to a litter of tiny black puppies. A couple of days later we encouraged her to come out with us for a walk, to give her a breath of fresh air before she resumed her maternal

My Dog, my Friend

duties. All was fine at first: new mother Millie was clearly happy to revisit her old haunts, sniffing at tufts of grass and padding around under the trees. But after ten minutes or so she suddenly sat down in front of me and stared into my face. I knew she was saying she had to get back to her babies, so I told her I quite understood and turned homeward. Millie bounded ahead of me up the path, back to the basket of puppies she knew needed a lick and a nestle into her warm, milky body.

I had never forgotten how clearly she had got her message across, and this time, too, it was obvious she was determined to stop us in our tracks because something was wrong. So, in spite of the sunshine, the bright leaves and the blackberries tempting us to walk on, we turned around and returned to the car, with Millie trailing behind us this time. When we arrived at the car we saw that one of the windows had been smashed where a thief had broken in and rummaged through the car, obviously hoping for something more valuable than old chocolate wrappers. He must have been disturbed by Millie's ferocious barking, and ran off, empty-handed. We hugged Millie and told her how clever she was, so thrilled by her guardian angel exploit that we couldn't be too upset about the broken window.

Years later, when my late husband, Desmond Wilcox, died, the whole family was devastated. Arthur, the Labrador, was mystified at first, unable to understand why Desi had gone. But with that wonderful, canine psychic instinct he would quietly seek out each of us, whoever was feeling the most miserable at any one moment, and snuggle up to us.

Esther and Desmond with Marmite and Millie

I remember him sitting with his head in my daughter's lap; then he would stretch out over my feet. It was strangely healing to pat his tummy, feel the gaze from his steady brown eyes, gently pull his soft ears. Somehow, he comforted all of us, reaching deep down to our unhappiness in a way no words could have done, and silently taking away some of the pain.

Alas, Millie and Arthur are no

longer with us, but they taught me the value of a dog's friendship. This has been described as unconditional love, which makes it sound rather soppy, and I prefer to think of it as intuitive love: a sensitive, wordless love which finds a way of communicating heart to heart. The bereaved, the grieving, the pressurised, the hopeless find consolation in the friendship of a dog. Those with the least – homeless, penniless rough sleepers, dwellers in cardboard cities – still own dogs, for that tough little mongrel is the one being who still needs them, rates them, loves them.

The loneliest individuals will reach out to a dog. A hospital patient in a geriatric ward will smile when a charity like Patdog brings a dog to visit. My current work for The Silver Line Helpline has shown me the intense loneliness that some older people can suffer, even when they are surrounded by others – when, for example, in residential care or sheltered housing. I believe that these people should be encouraged to have dogs, either as pets or as visitors, because – as I have discovered – the best cure for loneliness is a dog.

Best known for producing and presenting the TV consumer programme That's Life! *for 21 years, Esther still launches herself into risky reality shows, from* I'm a Celebrity *to* Strictly Come Dancing.*
However, she now spends most of her time working with many different charities, including Samaritans, having founded 'ChildLine' in 1986 (of which she is President and Trustee), and currently creating and chairing 'The Silver Line,' a helpline for isolated and vulnerable older people.

My best mate, Charlie

Steve Trigg

As an adult I always wanted a dog but work commitments made it impossible to be a responsible owner. I had a lovely house in Abingdon, a fantastic job with Npower, and a brand new BMW. But due to a really messy relationship breakdown I ended up losing everything. Losing my job hurt the most as I loved my job, and it was really good money.

I ended up in the night shelter in Oxford where drink and drugs soon took over my life – anything to ease the pain. But the drink was getting out of control: I was drinking at least seven litres of sherry a day, and spending £50 a day on drugs.

A girl that I knew had a few dogs, and one of them was having puppies so I decided to buy one, and I named her Charlie – she is a Collie cross. To be honest, I wanted a dog to help me make money for the drink and drugs. Now that's not the case. I think the world of Charlie: she is such a lovely, friendly little thing and I adore her, but I was in a bad place with the drink.

Charlie got pregnant by another homeless dog called Freddy, which was the last thing I wanted (I was living in a tent at the time). Anyway, she went into

Steve and Charlie

My Dog, my Friend

labour and had ten puppies. I thought "My God, how can I look after all these dogs?" so I packed in the drink and drugs to take care of my dog. That's been two years now of being clean from heroin and dry from the drink. I found loving homes for all the puppies. Me and Charlie now have a nice little flat, which I've lived in for 18 months, and we work together selling *The Big Issue* to help pay rent, bills, and buy food.

My dog turned my life around. I would probably be dead by now if it wasn't for her. We spend every minute together. I never thought a dog could have such a powerful influence on my life. Charlie saved my life, now it's my turn to save hers.

Charlie is suffering from cancer of the blood, and she is only 3½ years old. But she is responding to treatment – a steroid called prednisolone and another drug called atopica, which is costing £110 per fortnight, which, luckily, Dogs Trust is paying for. To show my thanks I put a thankyou in the *Oxford Times* to show how grateful we are for all its help.

So has my dog saved and changed my life? Oh yes! And if you are ever in Oxford town centre you will find us outside M&S.

Big Issue, anyone?

Steve Trigg, 49, and his dog, Charlie, sell The Big Issue *outside Marks and Spencer in Oxford. From having a successful career and his own home, Steve has been homeless and addicted to alcohol and heroin. In the last few years he has got himself clean and housed, and is now looking to get back into his previous line of work.*

The Big Issue believes in offering a hand up, not a hand-out. Vendors buy the magazine for half the cover price, and sell it at full price for a profit. There is support available for vendors like Steve, to help them access, among other things, addiction support, health and mental health care, and accommodation support.*

Barney

Bob Alper

We made a dumb mistake naming him.

He came to us from the mean streets of Puerto Rico where they toss stray dogs off bridges. This guy was more fortunate: his mother was killed, but the litter, aged about three weeks, was found by a rescue group that hand-fed them, wormed and neutered them, and flew them to New Hampshire where, in foster care, they called him 'Mr French.' We were never fans of the TV show *Family Affair*, so naming our dog after their butler didn't resonate.

We adopted him at six months, and when all the members of our family could finally agree on the name Barney, that was it. To my horror, a few weeks later, when it was too late to change, I realized that George Bush had named his dog Barney. But then I rationalized that the sins of the father are not necessarily passed on to – well – the family dog. So his name remained Barney, though his formal name, which, naturally, I registered with The American Mongrel Association, is 'Dr Bernard K Feindog.'

We live in a small Vermont town where some people know me (I'm a rabbi who has been a full-time stand-up comic for 27 years), and more people know Barney. When I'm not travelling, Barney is my constant companion.

He's a handsome, mid-size guy, about 60 pounds. Asked his breed, I have a few answers, depending on my mood and my estimation of the inquisitor's sense of humor. Sometimes, I say he's a 'purebread mongrelian.' Other times I explain that he enjoys fetching apples, and is, apparently, a 'golden delicious retriever.' Or I just say he's a combination Boxer and Chihuaha. As if.

For Barney, pretty much every day is Hallowe'en, with him receiving treats at every location. As I run my errands, he tags along. No leash needed. First, the post office, where he trots in, sits, and waits for the postmaster to pass his biscuit across the counter. Then the bank's drive through. My receipt is always accompanied by a biscuit. I smile and usually say, "Thank you. And – ummm – could I have one for the dog, too?"

When I go to the pharmacy, they scold me if, for some reason, Barney is not with me. I particularly enjoy walking in, hearing people call out "Hello, Barney!" and then having the clerk ask my name.

As a comedian, I love to make people laugh. And as a rabbi, I know well that there's more to laughter than pleasant diversion. There's a holiness in laughter as it lifts the spirit and heals the body. It's fun hanging out with Barney,

© Emily Katzenstein

© Sam Khan

Barney and Bob

and he and I are very much partners in trying to bring informal joy to the people we encounter.

Especially with a couple of Barney's tricks.

His best is one where he'll roll onto his side and lay still when I ask, "Barney: would you rather be a Republican or dead?"

And then there's his religious sensitivity. He's Jewish, of course. If I hold a treat in front of him, he'll go for it, until I quietly say, "Treif," which means 'not kosher.' He'll immediately suspend his quest and wait while I carefully examine the item, pretend to change my mind, and say, "Oh, wait. It's kosher." Chomp.

And he's respectful of other religions, even Christianity. Treat offered, I might suddenly caution, "Tasty." He'll ignore the food, until, once again, I examine it and pronounce, "Bland!" At which point he'll devour it.

What Barney and I do is our version of street theatre. Some don't quite 'get' it, but most are amused, and they occasionally tell me that our encounter provided a needed break from a tough day. Those are the responses I love. And Barney? He loves it too.

As long as there are treats involved.

85

Bob Alper is an ordained rabbi who served large congregations for 14 years. In 1986, he transitioned to full-time comedy, appearing across North America and England. He's also the founder of The Laugh In Peace Tour, and has done over 400 shows with Muslim comedians. Bob's newest book, Thanks. I Needed That *has just been released. www.bobalper.com.*

Dogs and Us
Tony Roper

When I was wee, like all wee boys I wanted a dog so I could have a special pal to play with.

I wanted someone who would sympathise with me when the grown-ups ganged up and persecuted me unfairly, which I was convinced frequently happened, especially when they would not capitulate and give me my way.

Finally, my mother did capitulate and I got a mongrel pup that I could not stop cuddling and stroking. I spoke to Glen (that was his name) as if he and I were one. For the first time in my short life

Tony and Frizby

I experienced what it was like to care for someone more than myself.

When I think back to that time I can now appreciate that special, almost spiritual, feeling that a dog can engender in two members of alien species. It is quite magical. Neither can speak to the other: they cannot discuss their day, what are their favourite colours, movies, taste in clothes, politics, etc, etc, but something happens when, for example, you are feeling low and your dog comes up and merely sits beside you. Something is released inside and you don't feel so alone. Your first instinct is to stroke his head or rub his back. The dog responds (always), and your troubles are eased, if not solved.

Glen was suddenly not there one day and I was beside myself (I was very young). My mother explained that because he was so special he had been selected from hundreds of other dogs to be trained by the army to help rescue miners who had been buried in a mine collapse. This was, of course, not true, Glen, in fact, had to be put down because he had distemper that was causing him to be very ill.

As the weeks went on I gradually accepted that Glen was not coming back, but it left a memory in my heart that could

My Dog, my Friend

only be eased by eventually, many years later, getting another dog.

Frizby was his name; he was a Bearded Collie. Isobel, my wife, gave me him for a Christmas present, and he was easily the best present I have ever had. From being a puppy who crapped and widdled all over the floor he grew to a friend who, due to some unfathomable inner clock, knew when it was nine o'clock at night and had to be given his walk, irrespective of rain, hail, sleet or snow, staring resolutely at me until I relented and headed for the door. This gave him permission to jump all over me and bark with glee at the prospect of the adventure we were both about to share in.

I gave him a home and food and walks, and Frizby gave me joy just by being there. When I came home I could hear his excited bark before I was out of the car door. When I opened the front door it was as if the second coming had arrived. He ran around me at least three times, then jumped up until I got down on my knees and indulged in a wrestling game, then brought me a selection of tugging toys to choose from for our next game. It would always end with his front paws on my shoulders as we had a final hug before Isobel fed the both of us.

Isobel got the same treatment, of course, when she came into the house, but she did not indulge in the rough and tumble, and Frizby had to make do with a toy being thrown, which he was duty-bound to bring back. It was, however, Isobel who had the patience to teach him every trick he knew: no mean feat as – despite being extremely lovable – he was also a wee bit dim where dog tricks were concerned.

As the years went by it became frighteningly obvious to us that our beloved pal was suffering with crippling arthritis, and would have to be released from his agony.

It fell to me to give him his last ride in the car to the vet. He went away very peacefully, and it broke my heart that I would never feel his warmth or see his head cock to the one side, looking as if he was trying to understand what I was on about again. I still would not have missed for anything the experience and privilege of having him in our lives.

Frizby and Glen gave me proof that there exists in dogs an in-built ability that releases a need in most humans to care for another species without any material reward being expected. A trait not found as a rule in other carbon forms on the planet. Throughout history mankind has been cruel and heartless, but how much worse would we be if not for our friend, the dog?

Tony has been a household name since the 1970s, starring in top-rating television shows that include Scotch and Wry, Naked Video, Only an Excuse, *and playing his alter ego Jamesie Cotter in* Rab C Nesbitt.

As a playwright he has written many sell-out shows, including Rikki and Me *in which he played the iconic Rikki Fulton, and* The Steamie, *which won him a Scottish BAFTA, and has played to sold out notices for the last 25 years.*

Tony is also the author of three novels: How I Found God And Why He Was Hiding From Me; One Deity At A Time Sweet Jesus, *and* The Steamie: A Novel, *all of which topped the Scottish best-selling list.*

In 2008 Tony was made a Doctor of Letters by Dundee Abertay University, and in 2010 was presented with a lifetime achievement award at the Great Scot awards.

A Forever Friend in Fido

Robert Vetere

Since my childhood I have always suspected that I felt better about myself – and life in general – whenever I was around my dogs. They have always been the ones with unconditional love; the ones who would listen without interruption or judgment to my every complaint. They never have a worse day than me; they never stay out late at night. And on and on. No matter how little or how much I travel the one who is always thrilled to see me return is my dog. With all of my time on the road, my wife finds a real companion to keep her company.

I am far from alone in feeling like this. Every day you will read or watch a story about how someone's bond with their dog has made an incredible difference in their life. The real magic, as it were, in all of this is it is not just a gut feeling that you are deriving a health benefit from your dog, it is fact. There is science explaining why soldiers suffering from post-traumatic stress disorder see improvement in their recovery when a dog is involved. Why autistic children find comfort and companionship when bonding with a dog. Why senior citizens enjoy a more comfortable life when around a dog.

They are amazing animals and I am thankful that they are always around to be my friends.

Bob Vetere currently serves as President & CEO for the American Pet Products Association (APPA), and oversees all association operations while collaborating with members, the Board of Directors, and other industry associations to support and further the success of APPA and its members. He is also the author of From Wags to Riches – How Dogs Teach Us to Succeed in Business & Life, *and resides with his wife and beloved dog, Dakota, in Connecticut.*

Bob and Dakota

One of god's greatest gifts

Mohamed Al Fayed

One of the greatest gifts god has given to humans is dogs: to guard us, give us pleasure, and to play with. I can't remember a time when they haven't been in my life.

When my brothers and I were growing up in Alexandria, in Egypt, we would play football on the beach every day, and our dog would always come with us. British troops from a nearby barracks often used to play with us. They loved our dog – I think it reminded them of home. Dogs can do that.

I have six at home – all different breeds – and the enormous welcome they give me when I get back always makes me smile.

Dogs have been a blessing to me: they are devoted in their loyalty and have a level of intuition that's almost like a seventh sense. It makes them wonderful companions.

They are teachers, too. It is in their nature to nurture, to love and protect – all fundamental principles in life – and for children to witness and experience this as they grow up helps to reinforce what we try to teach them as parents.

When my children were growing up, I loved to see them playing in the garden with the dogs. Their favourite was a Golden Retriever called Humphrey: he was a great comfort, and made their lives that extra bit special. My children are all grown up now with children of their own, and Humphrey is no more. It's a new chapter in our family's life. And I now take great delight in watching my grandchildren interacting with these beautiful, caring creatures. Because, just like children, they can make light when it may otherwise feel dark.

My Dog, my Friend

Mohamed enjoying time with his dogs

Mohamed Al Fayed is an Egyptian-born businessman and entrepreneur. He owns the Ritz Paris, but perhaps is best known for transforming Harrods into the world's most famous department store. He once had a Golden Retriever called Humphrey who was so clever and perceptive that the family decided to call him Sir Humphrey.

Life with Labradors

Fred MacAulay

We've had black Labradors since the day our daughter left primary school in 1998. Our first was Maisie and we added Poppy about five years later. Maisie lived till she was nearly 15, and we always thought she'd be the first to go, but sadly Poppy predeceased her as a result of a tumour. It was quite unexpected and, as with all owners, our hearts were broken. She had a general anaesthetic for a biopsy and, on discovering how advanced the tumour was, the vet advised that she be put to sleep there and then. I find myself still holding back a tear even as I write this.

Then Maisie died of old age in February 2013. Whilst this death was more expected, it was no less heartbreaking. But the point of this is that, despite the heartache all owners might feel at the loss of a dog, the good times far outweigh those sad days when they leave us.

When Poppy was five she had a litter and delivered seven pups: six boys (four black and two yellow), and a lovely bitch who we kept and called Izzy. So, for a few years we had three adult Labs careering around the house, causing mayhem occasionally, but generally giving back the love with which our three children showered them.

Shortly before Maisie died, we introduced our fourth bitch, Tiggie. Tiggie is quite different from the other three in nature: much more reserved and considered, but she's turning into a beautiful dog, and we look forward to maybe getting a litter from her in a couple of years' time. We've never considered having anything other than Labradors: they're great fun and always ready for a walk, which is the ideal way of getting us out of the house in all weathers.

So here we are now with two dogs in the house and the kids have all but departed, but the dogs love it when the kids all come home just as much as we do!

Fred MacAulay is one of Scotland's most famous comedians. He regularly appears on television, and every year he performs at the Edinburgh Fringe. He is also one of the best known voices on BBC Radio Scotland, hosting his own daily show for over 15 years. He has appeared, by invitation, in Australia, Hong Kong, America, Iceland and Iraq, and uninvited, in many other countries.

Our current two Labradors, Izzy (on the left) and Tiggie on a dreich day, drying out in front of the aga after our daily walk round the fields near our house. How lucky are we?

Gorgeous girls

Jude and Immie Brooks

My dogs – two past and one present – occupy very special places in my heart, and I am honoured that Jacki has asked me to write about them for this fascinating anthology about our dogs and what they mean to us.

Westie sisters Hubble and Hattie – namesakes of the publisher of this book – taught me what love for another species is, and now that they no longer walk with me in this life, how lucky am I that Imani – Immie (also known, on occasion, as Da Immster, Imanicricket, and Princess Tippytoes) – continues with the lesson: filling my life with love, laughter, and contentment.

Imani is especially special as she began life in Northern Cyprus: abandoned after giving birth to a litter of money-making puppies, and probably destined to live out her days in the English-run rescue centre there, if she hadn't happened to attract our attention one hot, sunny day some thirteen or so years ago.

But why don't I let her take up the tale ...?

"I never could have imagined leaving the island of my birth, and taking a very scary plane ride to begin a new life in the UK, but that's exactly what happened.

"Why ever my mum-to-be decided that, out of all of the lovely dogs at the rescue centre, it was me she wanted to give a forever home to I will never know, as I was a fairly pitiful sight, and too scared, at first, to go out on a walk with her. In fact, she carried me for a good part of the way to allow me to enjoy the freedom of not being caged, along with the other eight dogs who were walking with us. However, when she put me down, I ran back in the direction of the rescue centre, too scared to continue. Something, though, must have told me that this was a chance for me, and I ran back to her and the others. And lucky for me that I did as, on the walk, she decided she wanted to take me home with her ...

"And so, within the space of a week – and after much frantic arranging and long-distance calls to a quarantine kennel back home in the UK – I left my unhappy start in life and flew the 4000 miles to my new home in Dorset.

"The six months I then had to spend in quarantine were helped by visits from mum – two, and sometimes three, times a week – and we would have a lot of fun playing with toys that she brought me, which was all new to me. The quarantine rules were very strict: I wasn't allowed out of my kennel, so mum had to be locked in there with me. Very often the weather wasn't good enough to go out in the adjoining run, so we would sit together on the concrete dais that was my bed, and mum would brush me to get me used to being groomed, which I'd also never experienced before!

"Eventually, one fabulous day in May 2002, my 'sentence' was up and I was allowed out of quarantine.

"What I didn't know until that point, however, was that my mum and her partner already had two dogs – Westie sisters called Hubble and Hattie – and these two weren't very pleased to see me *at all*. Oh, we all got along okay, and there was never any fighting, but the sisters made it very plain that I was one dog too many at Winkle Cottage ...

"Nevertheless, my life was happy, and I was glad to be in England rather than Cyprus, where all the other dogs bullied me, and I never got enough to eat as I was too timid to fight back when others stole my food. Now, I had enough to eat, lots of treats, a fab garden to play in, and two walks a day. Yep, life was pretty damn good!

"Fast forward twelve years and now there's just mum and me at Winkle Cottage. Hubble and Hattie both died in 2007, at the good age of 14 years. I know mum has thought about getting another dog or – heaven help us – a cat (yuck!), but I think she knows that I might find that a bit difficult to get used to; anyway, it's really lovely with just the two of us.

"Mum still feels very sad about Hubble and Hattie, I know, but the fact

© Jude Brooks

Jude and Immie

that she's remembered them in a very special way – by naming an imprint after them that publishes books about animals which are designed to improve their lives, as well as encourage understanding and compassion for all species – has helped her feel better, and she knows her gorgeous girls would be thrilled to bits that the imprint is named after them!

"So now, as always, I go into the office every day with mum and 'help' her work on the Hubble and Hattie books. So far we've published 39, with many more planned. And, best of all, I'm actually pictured in several of them!"

95

Jude is co-owner of Veloce Publishing, parent company to the Hubble and Hattie imprint.
Launched in 2009, Hubble & Hattie books have the underlying objective to be of real benefit to the species they cover; at the same time promoting compassion, understanding and respect between and for all animals. Check out the H&H website – www.hubbleandhattie.com – to see the range.

Dogged devotion

Tim Dowling

I often correct people who refer to me in public as a dog lover. "I'm a dog owner," I say. "It's not the same thing." This is partly because I have two dogs, and I know that when I'm out walking them both there's a danger of me being mistaken for some kind of enthusiast. Getting the second one was not my idea; I objected, and was overruled. I like dogs, but I've also learned from experience that two is one dog too many.

As someone who works from home, I suppose their main compensating feature is that they provide me with constant, non-judgemental company. If there's a dog in the room, then technically I'm not talking to myself. If there are two dogs, then I'm basically chairing a meeting. But their devotion can be a little unhinged. They shadow me through the house all day long like close-protection bodyguards. They stare at my back while I work. If I stand up, they stand up. The little one, in particular, is so needy that it leaps in the air like a hooked marlin to greet me when I come back from the corner shop.

I'll admit I find all the attention overwhelming from time to time – especially when they approach you with a look in their eyes that says, "Let's do something! Now!" – but when they're asleep by the fire in winter, or in the sun in summer, I find their presence immensely comforting. It's at those times that I realise that the dogs love me the way I love my children: with an all-consuming intensity that is guaranteed to irritate the recipient eventually. On those occasions I resolve to be a bit more gracious about being the target of their lavish affections.

As I said, I like dogs, and I also know how sharper than a serpent's tooth it must be to have me as an owner.

Tim Dowling is a writer and columnist for The Guardian. *He has two dogs, Bridey and Nellie.*

90

Tim with close-protection bodyguards Bridey (lying) and Nellie

Putty in the dog's paws

Ian Hamilton

25 years ago I was introduced to my first guide dog, whose name was Ursula. Being blind was bad enough without having a dog who was lumbered with a name like that, so I re-named her Stella (don't ask!).

I've always found using a white cane slow and cumbersome; working with Stella for the first time was exhilarating as I moved smoothly round obstacles, and at a walking speed I had never experienced with a white cane.

I've now worked with six guide dogs, each with a character alarmingly different from the previous dog: the moody, the officious, the joker, and the Buddhist, to name a few. From a puppy the dogs take about 20 months to train, and at least a further year to settle down with their new blind owner.

In general, the public vastly overestimates a guide dog's abilities, assuming that he or she knows when it is safe to cross a busy road. But how can a dog judge the speed of a double-decker bus, for example?! At the end of the day, he's a dog who can be highly unpredictable, so it's my decision when to give my dog an instruction to turn down a street or cross a road. The most important thing to understand is that a guide dog is the only canine trained to disobey my command if he sees or senses danger: stopping at holes in the ground, and wheelie bins abandoned on the pavement, and also sitting and waiting for instruction at a kerb.

Being sentient animals rather than automatons, they are capable of exacting sweet revenge if corrected for doing something wrong, or something which they disagree with.

Stella, for example, if it was raining, and she didn't want to go out, would sulk, walk slower, and guide me through all the puddles on the pavement, as she lightly tip-toed around the edges, keeping her paws nice and dry, whilst I would be splashing my way through the deep end. Another dog would go on strike and throw himself to the ground, refusing to move.

My third dog was a different proposition to all of the others. Tim was a seven stone German Shepherd, with a personality to match … this was a dog to be reckoned with. He could swing from being a genius one minute to an idiot the next. Travelling on busy trains with Tim was fantastic, as he had a real physical presence that cleared seats quicker than you could blink, staring intently at passengers until they snapped and moved away. He also took control when

getting off the train. We would be ready as the doors opened, and as impatient passengers lunged forward to board they would come nose-to-nose with a mean-looking German Shepherd. I could feel his head turn slowly left and right as he scanned the platform as, very quietly, the crowd parted like the Red Sea. "That's ma boy!" I'd think, as Tim proudly guided me off the train and we'd be on our way.

With usual German proficiency Tim took his work very seriously, and was a master at weaving in and out of shoppers and *Big Issue* sellers. If anyone dared to get in the way they would be subjected to a cold, sharp nose up the bottom. You can imagine the reactions: shrieks, cursing, shopping bags falling to the ground, pedestrians leaping into the air like rockets. Amidst all the chaos Tim would change up a gear, and, with me hanging on to the harness, circumnavigate the pile-up and accelerate into the outside lane. Brimming with confidence we would zoom down the street and turn down a quieter side road, allowing me to catch my breath.

But an empty pavement bored Tim, and, catching sight of a lone approaching pedestrian, he would begin to walk towards the unsuspecting person, despite there being plenty of room on the pavement, and ample space to pass. By the time the three of us met, Tim would have forced the poor individual against the wall, actually leaning on him as we passed. Then Tim would simply swish his tail happily, moving back into the centre of the quiet pavement again as if nothing had happened.

My friend, Mark, got a new guide dog after his previous one retired, and I was so impressed when I learned that his dog had been trained to actually press the button at pedestrian crossings. On arriving at the crossing his dog lifts her front legs and presses the button with her snout. I've spent hundreds of pounds on gadgets to do this very job!

My recently-retired dog, Moss (black Labrador now 13 years old), just loved to upstage me by posing for the camera when I was interviewing politicians: one particular editor insisted that Moss featured in every TV report! On one unforgettable occasion I was chairing a social work conference in Edinburgh, and was only halfway through my opening speech when I heard Moss loudly groaning and yawning under the table. Undaunted, I carried on, but soon noticed that people were first sniggering and then laughing out loud. Someone whispered in my ear … Moss had crawled, commando-style, from under the table and had begun to empty the second speaker's handbag! Very deliberately, one piece at a time, the contents of her life were displayed for all to see.

But how can I correct a dog, when the audience is just putty in his paws …?!

99

Renton is a German Shepherd who guides Ian Hamilton around as he does his job as a BBC reporter for BBC TV and radio news in Scotland. They are regulars on TV, and Ian has made a couple of documentaries in which Renton featured prominently.

Remembering Jackie

William McIlvanney

I've been a dog lover all my life. I had no choice. My father had dogs. If that makes it sound like a disease, that's probably fair enough. I don't ever remember him actually buying a dog. It just seemed to be that every so often he developed a dog. I remember he and my mother came home at half-past ten one night from the pictures with a smooth-haired Fox Terrier. It had followed them when they got off the bus, my father said.

I believe him. He had an uncanny rapport with animals of all kinds. Dogs did sometimes follow him home. Jackie was one. It followed him home and stayed the night. It was returned to its owners and then came back to our house the same night. This happened so often that the owners told my father to keep it, since it had obviously decided where it wanted to live. That was Jackie. You didn't decide Jackie was your dog, Jackie decided you were his human.

Jackie was a brown and white mongrel, with a coat so rough and ill-fitting he looked as if he had borrowed it from a bigger dog and hadn't had the alterations done yet. He would be lucky if he stood a foot high but nobody had told him that. He thought Alsatians were a push-over.

In case that last fact gives you the wrong impression, Jackie was also the most intelligent dog I have ever come across. I kid you not, this was Wittgenstein with a tail.

Small example: Jackie used to travel everywhere on the bus, by himself. He simply jumped aboard and lay in the space under the stairs they used to have in the old buses, and got off at his stop. A neighbour once heard a passenger inform the conductress that there was an unaccompanied dog on the bus. "Aye," the conductress said. "That dog always gets this bus. Never been known to pay a fare yet, either."

When Jackie went shopping with my mother one day and she joined the queue for the bus that went in the direction of my grandmother's house, Jackie waited in an adjoining queue, for the bus that passed our street. My mother said he kept trotting down to her queue to stare at her quizzically, as if trying gently to suggest that she had lost her marbles. The bus for our house came first and Jackie got on it, standing briefly on the platform as it pulled away and staring back, before retiring to his reserved seat under the stairs. My mother couldn't swear to it but she thought he might have been shaking his head at her.

Badly wounded in a dog-fight, he

lay on his blanket without anaesthetic and let my father stitch him together with fuse wire. Not a sound. He healed well. When he reached an agonised old age and my father finally took him to the vet, Jackie lay watching my father with what looked like affection till the last sleep came. I suspect my father whimpered a bit but Jackie didn't. He was a philosopher to the end.

Jackie loved my father and my father treated him like a dog. That was the point. To treat a dog as if it is just a funny-shaped person with a very severe speech impediment is a kind of decadent colonialism, like trying to convert a happy native from his natural life to the dubious joys of civilised neurosis. Jackie may have had a kind of genius but it was a genius he could only express in his own ways, which included shoving his nose up very unsavoury places and leaving little messages in urine all over the place, and fighting other dogs and going on the hunt for very small bitches. It was what he did. He was a dog.

So, if we ever feel like getting a psychiatrist for our dogs, maybe we should get one for ourselves first. It should at least help us to realise that our need may be greater than theirs, that it may be our sense of us which is the problem, not the dog's sense of itself.

Remember Jackie. I know I will.

© Neil McIlvanney

101

William McIlvanney has been at the forefront of the Scottish literary scene for decades. Regarded as the godfather of 'Tartan Noir' (Scottish crime writing), he has received many awards, most recently in 2013 from the Saltire society in recognition of his outstanding contribution to Scotland's life and culture. In fact, Alex Salmond (First Minister of Scotland) has joked that William is responsible for his pursuit of a career in politics!

William's novel The Big Man was made into a film starring Liam Neeson, Billy Connolly, and Hugh Grant.

My granddog
Quintin Jardine

The boy, Canelo, was the runt of the litter. Sunny, his mum, was glad to see the back of him … literally. His name came from his colour as a pup, 'canela' being Spanish for cinnamon, although that lightened as he grew older. Today, he's showing some white around the whiskers.

He isn't mine, not directly: I call him my granddog. My stepson had decided from the start that he would keep one of the four pups, and Canelo landed the job by default, as the one that only a mother (and a granddad) could love. He's said to be a pedigree Labrador, but it was obvious from the start that he's a throwback to something. His legs and his tail are just a little longer than they should be, and he doesn't do the placidity of the Lab breed, being just a little on the nervous side. Also, I am not being unkind when I say that he is intellectually challenged. He's never even learned to scratch himself properly. His method is to stand on three legs, while clawing violently at himself with the fourth.

He is affectionate, though, in a slobbery way that once I couldn't stand in dogs. He's an inveterate licker, and shows that he cares by sitting in front of me and laying a humungous front paw on my leg. When I remove it, the other one replaces it. While this is happening, I look him in the eye, where I can see the undiluted, unmitigated, generous goodness of his soul.

What Canelo wants most of all is to make friends. He shouts his affection at everyone: at the people next door; at other dogs passing in the street, and on occasions in the past, joggers, when we were out walking.

That has been a problem. Canelo has never wanted simply to say 'hello' from a distance. He wants to do it close up, and not everyone appreciates a big gawky dog rushing towards them, or understands that his full-throated bark means, in fact, "Hi there, I'm Canelo! Who the hell are you?"

There was one occasion when he was around a year old, and lacking any proper discipline, when a fat bloke in a tracksuit and trainers was about to brain him with a rock, until he realised that, of the two of us, I was a lot more dangerous than the pup.

Since then we've reached an understanding. Canelo doesn't chase joggers, and I don't hit them.

As I say, he's not my dog, but he might as well be.

My Dog, my Friend

Eileen, Quintin's wife (and Canelo's Granny),
with Canelo

Once upon a … Quintin Jardine was born in Motherwell, Lanarkshire, but he escaped, and now lives in East Lothian and in Spain, with his wife and extended family. He is the author of 34 best-selling crime novels, all published globally by Headline. The most recent is Hours of Darkness, *the twenty-fourth to star his creation, Chief Constable Bob Skinner. His second, and slightly anarchic, series featured actor-detective Oz Blackstone, and ran to nine books. It ended with* For the Death of Me, *and was followed by* The Primavera Mysteries, *the fifth of which,* As Serious as Death, *was published in November 2013.*

    Amidst all of this, Quintin found time to produce a stand-alone novel, The Loner, *which he regards as one of his finest.*

My life with dogs

Julie Myerson

My first dog was a Scots Collie, a 'Lassie' dog. I was seven and I decided to call her Sparky. I trained her to knock tennis balls off carefully-aligned Ski yoghurt pots, to play tug of war with a slipper, and just once, I sat on the back doorstep and ate Winalot with her. I wanted to see what it was like to be her – to taste what she tasted; to see the world as she did.

But as I grew up, she became a less urgent and exciting presence. And when, at 16, I finally got kissed by a boy, it didn't seem very important that she was there too – sighing and creaking in her basket in the hall – while he and I stood, close and tense in the darkness. At university, I forgot all about her. When Mum phoned and told me she'd been put down, I don't think I cried.

For a long time, I had no dog. Then I turned 40 and told my husband we needed a dog. "We don't need a dog," he said. "A dog is the last thing we need. We can't even manage the kids, let alone a dog!" I should have listened. I didn't. I whined. Three months later, we got an eight-week-old Border Collie.

Betty was headstrong, neurotic and obsessive. Also passionately affectionate, clever and unique. Most of all, though, she was never trained. She quickly realised that a command from me was no more than a suggestion, a possibility. But she changed our lives for the better, taking the family to good places both literally (outdoors) and metaphorically (animals teach kids about mess, love, compromise and, ultimately, death). When she died, my husband and I wept. "That's it," we said. "We won't get another dog."

But two years later there was a dog-shaped hole in our lives. We went to a Border Collie breeder and Rabbit was the first dog we saw – in a pen at the front, forlorn and surrounded by Poodles. "It's because she gets bullied," the breeder said. "I daren't leave her with the other dogs." She went on to show us some of these other dogs, but it was pointless: I already loved Rabbit.

Rabbit – the only name the whole family could agree on – is unlike any dog I've known. Timid, intense, adoring and possessed of a rare stillness. And, though I've tried hard to be a better trainer, the truth is she does the right thing (mostly) not out of obedience, but because she's just a genuinely nice person.

Rabbit has brought a sweetness to our lives, giving us back a sense of ourselves that is both reassuring and energising. You can't feel sad or bad for very long with a dog. Most of all, when

© Chloe Myerson

Julie and Rabbit

your confidence is at its lowest, when you feel battered – by life, death and (especially) other humans – a dog will shove her nose in your hand and tell you, with conviction and feeling, what a really good person you are.

Julie Myerson is the author of 13 books, most recently The Quickening. *Though she never sets out to write about dogs, they have crept into a number of her novels, and their presence – on the page, as in life – always seems to illuminate the human characters.*

Magnus
Sally Beamish

you were mainly
very smelly

but also the gentlest
the daftest
huge golden dog

we fetched you from your mother
children rapturous in the back of the car
you nestled in my lap
and I was smitten

you lay across my feet
while I worked
kept me at my desk

you learnt to ring a bell to go out
because you wouldn't bark

you chased rabbits
but whimpered and fled
when one turned to face you
and once
we found you cradling a litter of eight
between your front paws
unharmed

sleeping,
you let the hens walk over your back
into the kitchen

you got wedged in the doorframe
with a stolen French loaf
in your soft jaws

you lay against the front door
just to be sure
who was in
and who was out

your heart gave up
when I left
mine mended
but yours never did

the last time I groomed you
I saved a handful of golden hair
to remember your smell

©Tom Kidd

Sally and Magnus

Sally Beamish is one of Britain's leading composers, whose music is performed internationally by orchestras, including the Minnesota Orchestra and the London Symphony Orchestra, and by legendary soloists, including Branford Marsalis and Steven Isserlis.

She was offered a choice of pets for her sixth birthday, but misguidedly chose a malevolent rabbit; after which she longed to own a dog until she finally acquired Magnus in 1998.

My relationship with dogs

Marty Becker

Holding the fur of a dog named Shep as he trotted across the lawn of our southern Idaho farm is my earliest memory. Who would have known that, from that point forward, I would literally be side-by-side with dogs throughout my personal and professional life? Maybe it was obvious from that very moment. Looking back now, it certainly seems that way to me.

I grew up in a time when the human-animal bond blossomed. Before the 1960s, Americans had proximity to dogs but not intimate contact: our lives intersected randomly but weren't intertwined. We wanted canine companions, but didn't know we needed them. I was there when it all changed – dare I say – furever?

A half-century ago, many dogs had a role that was strictly utilitarian: they hunted, herded, ratted, alerted and guarded. Then millions of backyard dog houses suddenly became obsolete as 'our' houses became 'their' houses, too. Our doors opened to welcome dogs inside, and we discovered that dogs could do more for us than just work at the jobs we'd given them. We laughed at their antics, smiled as they followed us like shadows, and felt the stresses of the day leave us as we sat side-by-side on the couch (or nose-to-nose in bed) and

connected with them. In this flowering of what I simply call 'The Bond,' we came to appreciate that the greatest gift of our canine companions was in their amazing capacity for emotional support.

Dogs provide us with unconditional love, limitless affection, and to-die-for loyalty. As we allowed ourselves to see this, our relationship with them changed over just a few decades from animal to pet, to family member, to now, in many cases, describing them as our children and calling ourselves their moms and dads. Research validates this: for many of us, pets act like and are regarded as children. That's no surprise for those of us who have continued to baby talk them through the geriatric phase, dress them up or kiss them goodnight.

While we always knew having pets around made us feel good, only in the last 25 years have we really understood just how good pets are for us. I think I was aware of this before many, having written *The Healing Power of Pets* just after the dawn of the new millennium. For that award-winning book, I discovered the research that validated the human-animal health connection which millions had already experienced, witnessed or intuited. From seemingly miraculous feats such as dogs detecting cancer and seizures, improving IQ scores, lowering serum cholesterol levels or reducing the risk of having a heart attack or increasing the chances of surviving one, I added documentation of what we already knew dogs could do such as lowering blood pressure, reducing stress, blunting chronic pain, soothing post-traumatic stress disorder, and elevating mood.

This potent medicine, soft fur and all, was already in around two-thirds of all US households – and now lives in even more. The cure is trusted and easily administered: I think we all agree having a pet is a medicine that's easy to take. What would you rather have when you're sick, sad or sore: a drug or a dog?

As the shadows begin to lengthen in my career and I look back at all the dogs I've had personally; the thousands I've touched as a veterinarian; the ones I've helped in shelters or the ones we've showcased on TV or in social media, my main observation is why we aren't even more in awe and appreciation of the gifts of The Bond. We've helped pets, and they've helped us even more. This affection connection isn't parasitic or win/lose: it has always been symbiotic – win/win.

When you think of bond, you think of connection or coherence. That's what the human-animal bond is. We cohere, are connected, cohabit. For me, the glue that forms The Bond with our family pets got stronger with each passing day, with each pet I saw in the veterinary hospital

Marty with Bernie

that left protected, treated, healed and always loved, or with the passionate interaction between other pet owners and their pets during the time we got to celebrate together this amazing covenant or uniting force.

We give dogs food, shelter and sometimes clothing (yes, even I do this!), supplemented generously with the time we can spare and the love we can share. Dogs, in return, give us unconditional love, limitless affection, and to-die-for loyalty, turn up our lips in smiles and join us unfailingly when we turn down our beds at night.

Without a doubt, this Bond is the best deal the human race has ever made.

109

Dr Marty Becker – 'America's Veterinarian' – is perhaps best known for his regular appearances on ABC's Good Morning America and on Animal Radio, and as the author of 22 books that have sold more than 7 million copies, including three New York Times best-sellers. He has lectured at every veterinary school in the United States, and has been named Companion Animal Veterinarian of the Year by the Delta Society (now Pet Partners), and the American Veterinary Medical Association. Marty practises, when his schedule allows, at two veterinary hospitals in north Idaho because he loves veterinary medicine, pets, and the people who care for them.

She snuggles up.
I adore her.

She looks out for me.
She is devoted.
She seems to know my every need.

Side by side we are strong.
I miss her when we are apart.
I love her.

I think we are alike, her and me.
Sometimes I behave like she is my
own flesh and blood.

She smells of the outdoors.
Of almonds.
Of lavender, sometimes.

She says I smell
of freshly baked bread.
People laugh when she says that.

They say
Dogs don't smell of freshly baked bread.

Looka does, she says.

Jacki Gordon

TALK TO US

If things are getting to you.

Talk to us any time you like, in your own way, and off the record – about whatever's getting to you.

📞 **08457 90 90 90*** ⬅

✉ **jo@samaritans.org**

🌐 **www.samaritans.org**

👁 **visit us** – find your nearest branch on our website

SAMARITANS

Samaritans is a registered charity.
*Please see our website for latest call charges.

Amazing dogs.
Transforming lives.

Lorna and her canine partner Eli are an incredible team.

Eli, like all our dogs, helps Lorna achieve so much in her daily life.

 Canine Partners

 caninepartners   @canine_partners

Canine Partners for Independence. A Charitable Company Limited by Guarantee. Registered in England No. 2516146.
Charity Commission Registered No. 803680. Scottish Registered Charity No. SC039050.
Registered Address: Canine Partners, Mill Lane, Heyshott, Midhurst, West Sussex GU29 0ED
T: 08456 580 480 E: info@caninepartners.org.uk

FRSB
give with confidence